# Sir Thomas Lawrence

1769–1830

Michael Levey

National Portrait Gallery, London
exhibition at 15 Carlton House Terrace, London sw1

Published for the exhibition held from
9 November 1979 to 16 March 1980 at the
National Portrait Gallery Exhibition Rooms,
15 Carlton House Terrace, London SW1

Exhibition Organizer John Hayes
Exhibition Designer Joe Pradera

© Michael Levey, 1979
ISBN 0 904017 32 x (paperback)  0 904017 31 1 (hardcovers)
Published by the National Portrait Gallery, London WC2H 0HE

Catalogue edited by Mary Pettman
Designed by Roger Huggett/Sinc
Printed in England by Balding and Mansell

*Cover* Mrs Wolff   (no.29)

*Sir Thomas Lawrence*

*Pope Pius VII*, detail  (no.38)

# CONTENTS

# Foreword

Lawrence has always been accepted as one of the great figures of the Regency. Already in 1790, when he was scarcely twenty-one, Sir Joshua Reynolds had acknowledged him as his successor in the art, the painter who would accomplish 'all that I have failed to achieve'. Reynolds was right in his prediction. Lawrence was to dominate portrait painting in England for forty years, and on his return from his triumphant 'mission' abroad to complete the great series of canvases which now adorn the Waterloo Chamber at Windsor, it was to find on landing at Dover that he had been elected President of the Royal Academy in succession to West. It seems unfair that he should also have been handsome, charming, and lionized by society; his love affairs with the Siddons sisters, Maria and Sally, have become part of the romantic legend. Yet Lawrence was a far more complex character than is often supposed. His romanticism was tempered by prudishness. He was more solitary than sociable. In spite of Farington's strictures about his neglect of his pupil, Lane, he was a highly diligent President of the Academy and the numerous long letters of advice extant testify to his concern for his fellow artists. Above all, ultimately he cared only for art; he was far from being just a fashionable portraitist. Often now accused both of flattery and bravura, he agonized over every detail in his portraits, which, unlike Reynolds, he executed entirely with his own hand. His eye was sharp. Nothing on the walls of the houses he visited escaped his scrutiny, and the passionate enthusiasm with which he pursued the acquisition of old master drawings, one of the most fabulous collections ever brought together, verged on obsession, contributing in no small measure to the disastrous state of his finances.

It has been a special source of pleasure to me that my colleague Michael Levey, Director of the National Gallery, who has for so long been an ardent admirer of Lawrence, should have agreed, at a time when he has been exceptionally busy, to select and catalogue this exhibition. I am greatly indebted to him for the care and thought he has given to this task. We must all be grateful to him for his insight. I wish also to express my gratitude to Joe Pradera for the characteristic practicality and sense of period which he has brought to the elegant setting for the exhibition, no less to Roger Huggett for his skill in designing this catalogue.

As Mr Levey says in his eloquent introduction, the exhibition has a very particular purpose: to demonstrate Lawrence's astonishing gifts both as painter and draughtsman. This would not have been possible without the wholehearted support of so many owners. Her Majesty The Queen has graciously lent no fewer than five works of the first importance from the Royal Collection. Her Majesty Queen Elizabeth The Queen Mother has graciously allowed us to borrow a previously unknown portrait drawing of George IV, museums in the United States have been outstandingly generous and, in one case, self-sacrificing, and owners in this country have been equally so. The Trustees and I are deeply grateful to them all.

JOHN HAYES
Director, National Portrait Gallery
June 1979

# ACKNOWLEDGEMENTS

My prime debt must be to Dr John Hayes, Director of the National Portrait Gallery, who generously – perhaps bravely – invited me to organize this exhibition. His keen interest and support have been much appreciated by me.

I felt particularly honoured by the commission, having long dreamt of an exhibition of Lawrence's work which should receive international support and do justice, at last, to his great gifts. Although one or two of his finest portraits (eg figs. 3 and 4) cannot unfortunately ever be lent, and although one or two English private owners declined to foster the repute of the artist and the pleasure of the public, the response from most owners was overwhelmingly positive, thoughtful and helpful. To all lenders I am profoundly grateful.

The scope of the exhibition is self-evident. It concentrates on examples of what I believe to be Lawrence's best work, though inevitably it is only a selection of this. Nor was selection always easy. From the first, however, I felt no attempt should be made to include paintings other than portraits and that stress should be laid on those portraits Lawrence himself chose to exhibit. Conversely, for the drawings – altogether a more private aspect of his art – it seemed good to indicate their wide range of subject-matter as well as style.

I have been greatly aided by all the hard work undertaken by members of the National Portrait Gallery staff, especially Miss Jacquie Meredith who not only assembled the pictures and drawings but kept me in touch with lively progress reports, and Miss Mary Pettman who has sympathetically guided this catalogue through the press. I am also most grateful to the designer of the catalogue, Mr Roger Huggett. To the exhibition designer, Mr Joe Pradera, I am indebted for his imaginative skill.

In preparing this catalogue I have incurred many debts. I must thank those who kindly gave me useful indications and answered various queries: Sir Geoffrey Agnew; Mr Hugh Brigstocke; Miss Maureen Duffy; Mr Everett Fahy; Mr John Gere; Mr John Ingamells; Sir Oliver Millar; Monsieur Pierre Rosenberg; and Dr Christopher White, who also spared time to read the whole typescript. I must thank too Mr William H. Wilson, Curator of the Ringling Museum, Sarasota, for his helpful interest and for information. In Dublin Dr James White, Director of the National Gallery of Ireland, was outstandingly helpful in many ways, and I am most grateful for his friendly interest and aid. Mrs Alice Mackrell very kindly provided comments on the dress worn by some of the sitters. I am greatly indebted to the researches of Mr Philip Vainker, who has carried out a detailed survey of newspaper critiques of Lawrence during his lifetime, a project largely funded by the Paul Mellon Centre for Studies in British Art; Mr Vainker's researches are gratefully utilized in the entries. At the National Gallery I am grateful for the interest and help of several colleagues, and for practical assistance as well from Miss Angelina Morhange and Miss Sheila Reid, the latter temporarily adding 'Lawrence' to already heavy secretarial tasks. I must also thank the Chief Photographer, Miss Lucy Close, and her staff, for some expert help. Mrs Grace Ginnis undertook the typing of the catalogue, and once again I warmly acknowledge her speed, efficiency and interest. For permission to quote from the Lawrence manuscript material at the Royal Academy of Arts, I am indebted to the Academy.

A special debt is owed to Dr Kenneth Garlick. As the author of the standard scholarly works on Lawrence, his name naturally recurs constantly throughout this catalogue; but my gratitude to him is more extensive and personal. He generously discussed the selection, gave valuable advice, especially over the drawings, and also lent me a portion of his own photographic material. The only tribute I can offer in recognition of his scholarship and his kindness – two qualities not always combined – is the dedication to him of this catalogue.

M.L.
London, July 1979

# INTRODUCTION

The purpose of any serious exhibition should be not merely to show but to demonstrate something. In the present instance what is to be demonstrated is the art of Lawrence; and few English artists are more in need of such a demonstration. Further, with Lawrence it is only through an exhibition that there can come extensive appreciation of his art.

The museums and galleries of this country are, with one or two exceptions, notoriously lacking in fine examples of Lawrence's work. Many of his best paintings, and some of his most sensitive drawings, remain in private hands, with the families for whom they were done. Other fine paintings long ago left England and are now dispersed, particularly in America. Assembly of his work from these varied sources is therefore the first essential; but there exists another handicap to greater understanding and appreciation of the artist.

His is, unfortunately, a very famous name. He has suffered from fame at least as much as other artists from obscurity, and it is a far harder thing to be rescued from. Along with great fame, beginning early on in his brilliant career, Lawrence has suffered – also beginning early on – from disapproval, reservations and characteristically native unease before the spectacle of artistry as stylish as his. The idea of Lawrence as an accomplished but superficial, flattering and even sentimental portraitist is a familiar one, now deeply rooted. Although he was neither a pupil nor a follower of Sir Joshua Reynolds, being, not unexpectedly, an utterly different artist, and of a different generation, with his own highly charged genius, he had to endure until the end of his life comparisons with Reynolds which automatically assumed the superiority of the older man. That Lawrence drew with an instinctive ability Reynolds could never approach, and handled oil paint with a masterly delight in the medium which Reynolds was incapable of experiencing, proved no recommendation with the majority of Lawrence's contemporaries and has not much helped him since – at least in England.

Until quite recently commentators and biographers treated his art with appalling condescension and his period with almost total incomprehension. In his polished manner, his social success, his dazzling virtuosity, he seemed to incarnate all that they distrusted about the Regency, an awkward, interim age supposedly lacking at once in eighteenth-century sense and Victorian sensibility. Nor, probably, have attitudes to Lawrence much changed, though expression of them may have become a little more sophisticated. His artistic virtuosity is as undeniable as his widespread social success; it fails to fit comfortably into the tradition of English painting, any more than does his progress across Europe, being fêted and patronized in the capitals of Vienna, Rome and Paris.

Very early did Lawrence's reputation start to suffer because of his great natural gifts. Before he was twenty-one an exactly contemporary painter, Martin Archer Shee, was writing sharply and unenviously to his own brother in Ireland: 'I cannot conceive who could so much have misinformed you about Lawrence. He is the very reverse of what he has been represented . . . [he is] one of the most laborious, industrious men in his profession . . .' Even today, when we have perhaps learnt not to equate too hastily extreme accomplishment with absence of thought or work, it still comes possibly as a surprise to read Lawrence's words in mid career about being 'as much the slave of the picture I am painting as if it had living, personal existence, and had chained me to it'. By itself that simple and quite private statement suggests someone approaching his art not as a slick society pet but with all the obsessive conviction of Ingres or Cézanne.

And there are plenty of other observations by Lawrence to show how passionately he was devoted to his art – leaving aside the most convincing of testimonies residing in the works themselves. It was part of his skill that they should not look laboured, however painfully he had worked on them; as he wrote to one of his more aesthetically discriminating patrons, Sir Robert Peel, 'the appearance of facility is not undesirable'. Yet he really toiled to achieve the image that he wanted to create – something beyond mere likeness – so as to leave the canvas permanently reverberating under the impact of a vitality not natural but artistic. He frankly declared that the result should be a work of the imagination, by being more beautiful than the reality on which it was based; and this was not forced on him by a need or wish to flatter. It helps to understand him a little to realize that he deliberately aimed at this effect – one which would probably have seemed eminently respectable if his subject-matter had been other than commissioned portraits. Breakfasting with his young nephew a few months before he died, Lawrence quoted the passage from Aristotle's *Poetics* where poets are told they ought to imitate good portrait painters who while preserving a resemblance yet make it more beautiful; and he said that he would like that dictum written up in letters of gold over the door of his studio, 'for he had constantly followed what it enjoined'.

Of all the people who knew Lawrence and looked at his work none was more perceptive in his appreciation of a fellow-artist than Delacroix. He met Lawrence in London and may then have seen the portrait of Pope Pius VII (no.38); when a mezzotint of it was published he wrote an absorbing article in the *Revue de Paris* for June 1829. Among other points, he emphasized how with Lawrence, 'malgré l'apparente facilité de sa manière, rien n'est plus consciencieux que son travail'. Many years later he told a friend that Lawrence sent him an eight-page letter in response, and this was taken from him by an autograph-hunter before he had fully digested it (a considerable loss to Lawrence studies).

Lawrence had used a particularly revealing phrase when he spoke of a picture having for him 'living, personal existence', because the subject of his art was living people. Each portrait presented a challenge – not to gain a good likeness (he had rarely any difficulty there) but to distil on to canvas the essence of *his* response to the sitter. That was something far more ambitious; it extended from the clothes worn to the setting in which he chose to present the person, and at its heart of course was the impact of the given personality on his tautly receptive, nervously keen sensitivity.

Ultimately, his life was peopled by the beings of his imaginative recreation far more than by ordinary individuals. For all his great social gifts, he became noted for his failure to be social, to entertain or establish around him the sort of convivial circle in which Reynolds had relaxed. Lawrence's large house was finally filled only by the hundreds (literally) of canvases of individuals to whom he had begun to give artistic existence (fig.1); and even those that appeared fully realized, completed, were often retained by him and were still in his studio at his death. In a way perhaps they could never be 'finished'; he never quite stopped having something more to express, while in reality the person might well have altered, grown old, even died.

Princess Lieven thought she was making a joke at Lawrence's expense, though she had briefly stumbled into artistic awareness, when she described how in his studio the artist treated such full-length portraits as those of Pope Pius VII, the Tsar (no.35) and George IV (no.33) 'as he would treat the originals if he were their major-domo!' The role of Lawrence, however, was to be not their servant but their master. It was through him that they possessed, in paint, that extraordinary vivacity and allure which exceed – and are meant to exceed – anything in nature. In art it was he who ordered their lives down to the last detail. During one of the numerous sittings given him by Pius VII, he noticed that a ring was missing from the Pope's finger; Pius himself hastened to go and fetch it. Where his art was concerned, Lawrence notably failed to be obsequious to his most powerful

FIG.1 Lawrence's studio, *c*.1824. Engraved by F. C. Lewis after a drawing by Mrs Calmady (see no.41).

sitters. Already, aged only twenty and confronted by the commission for his first royal portrait, that of Queen Charlotte (no.3), he had asked the Queen to talk so as to animate her features; and her semi-snub to the young painter for presuming probably had little effect. 'Sir', he exclaimed to the Tsar as their first sitting drew towards a close, 'I *can't* be reasonable'; and when his friend Lord Stewart meaningfully glanced at him to concur with the Tsar's assumption that no more time was necessary, he immediately answered, '*much* more, Sir', (his own italics).

He would choose the colour of his sitters' clothes (cf no.32), and even at times the animal to accompany them: 'I think the dog I have selected probably better suited to my purpose', he told one patron – and under the silky tone there is a touch of artistic steel in the words 'my purpose', as well as concern to portray an exact animal no less than a person. He painted out the stripes on a sash worn by the Duke of Wellington because they were visually offensive ('never mind', said the Duke, 'they merely constitute me Generalissimo of the Armies of Spain'). A great lady arranging to sit enquired if she should wear a gown of black velvet, and apparently Lawrence agreed. Well he might, given his response to this sumptuous material, which is very much 'his', as silks and muslins are Gainsborough's. The expanse of Mrs Stratton's black velvet dress (no.25) and the rich red velvet of Charles Lambton's suit (no.42) are painted with a sensuous feel for texture quite foreign to, say, Reynolds, for whom drapery was a chore to be handed over to studio assistants. For Lawrence the sit of a coat collar, hard flash of buttons or jewels and soft fall of cashmere shawl are all part of the spell of a personality, to which he must do artistic justice. Nobody in England but Lawrence – young as he then was – could have painted so palpably Miss Farren's tightly gloved hand clasping the furry expanse of her huge muff on which a single pale blue ribbon is poised like an exotic butterfly (no.4).

When he died his studio contained, along with the hundreds of portraits, oddments of the sitters' personal belongings which he had required to study: the sword the Duke of

Wellington wore at Waterloo, Lord Combermere's military belt, the Marquess of Hertford's Garter star and a group of George IV's foreign decorations. The glittering precision of such details in Lawrence's pictures, like the heavily annotated drawing of an Uhlan soldier (no.82), shows how scrupulously he pursued – and enjoyed pursuing – minutely exact appearances.

To his contemporaries, and especially to his patrons, the slowness of Lawrence's progress in painting portraits was a constant cause of wonder – and complaint. They understood next to nothing about art (as is apparent from the majority of newspaper critiques of the period) and could have little sympathy with the struggles of an artist who seemed as materially successful as he was naturally gifted. He had been commissioned to execute a job, one for which he had usually been well paid, which made his delays the more inexplicable and reprehensible; all that was required was that he carry out his task.

A lesser artist – and one with less ambition – would have found it much easier to do so. What to Lawrence were, in words he emphasized in capital letters, 'the nervous difficulties' of confronting and portraying, for example, European sovereigns, ministers and statesmen, were of little concern to the society which employed him. *How* he achieved his effects was his own business, no more relevant than the expertise of the valets, tailors, farriers and tradesmen who variously ministered to other social needs. Indifferent to artistic murder, society echoed Macbeth in thinking it well that the deed were done quickly.

Some of Lawrence's delays arose from his temperament, with its alternating extremes of torpor and excitement; but that too was because he took his art so seriously. Like his carelessness and increasing detachment in non–artistic affairs, it shows how profoundly he was absorbed by, often also exhausted by, the demands he made on himself to capture his vision of a sitter. It was achieved only by hard labour. Nothing in a picture, he once wrote, 'is a matter of accident'.

In such a picture as that of Mrs Wolff (no.29) everything seems studied in a portrait which shows an unusually studious woman. It is more than a portrait in the conventional sense, for it conveys atmosphere at least as much as a likeness: a hint of sculpture gallery in its setting and the suggestion of study, by night, of great works of art (Michelangelo's Delphic Sibyl, from the Sistine ceiling). Mrs Wolff seems to have been intelligent as well as beautiful, and Lawrence has made special efforts to convey as much. She has passed from nature into art. Although her pose derives from Michelangelo it appears as if filtered through Parmigianino in its elongated, impossible grace and fluidity. Her long neck, her disproportionate arms and her anatomically incredible knee have been manipulated as much as the cool river of white satin that forms her dress and is set off, like fabric in a shop window, against the rich and partly patterned fiery reds of the background. Looking at the resulting picture, it is easy to believe that it took the artist many years to complete.

His tremendous technical gifts would have been sterile without the animating, as it were lubricating, fluid provided by his almost fevered sensibility. He was conscious of it, perhaps proud of it; certainly he remarked how Reynolds had been 'of a cold Temperament, a philosopher from absence of the Passions'. Lawrence felt intensely, whether it was the public events of his period like the death of Nelson or of Princess Charlotte ('an event in the great drama of life') or the humble, private incident of a coalman seen in the Strand weeping over his dog crushed accidentally under his own wagon wheel. When one evening in Paris he visited the cemetery of Père Lachaise his eye was caught by a woman kneeling, mourning at, as he noted, 'a small Tomb'. In Germany he saw the students drifting like Florentine Renaissance figures through the streets of Heidelberg, with its castle 'a dream, a relic of Ariosto, left by him to be once seen by Lord Byron . . .' Nearer home, and more simply, he could respond with no less intensity to the fishing boats putting off in a brisk gale at Hastings: that spectacle, he said, left 'very powerful impressions on one's senses and imagination'. And it is easy to see why he instinctively enjoyed, and possibly envied, Turner's art. Writing of landscape and nature, again to Sir Robert Peel, he confessed: 'I have always felt that I had some power in representing it'.

But for him it was quickly proved, and never altered, that nothing excited his imagination more than people. Around them crystallized all those associations of grandeur, history, intellect, beauty and pathos which he constantly experienced and which he sought to convey in the resulting portraits. They were bound to be more than mere likenesses of a child, an old lady, a soldier or a monarch because they possessed so much more meaning for the artist; they enshrined natural innocence and vivacity, dignity, bravery and wisdom – and those qualities in no contrived symbolic sense but just as Lawrence detected them as he gazed at each sitter. His art was a sort of mimesis, whereby he became each sitter in a way quite foreign to Reynolds. In Reynolds's portraits the sheer intelligence of the conception carries off the frequently clumsy, lack-lustre execution; the painter is as detached as a playwright moving among actors, but Lawrence is temperamentally one of them, emotionally keyed up, acutely responsive, concentrating on execution as he tries to absorb and express the vitality of each role. And at the end of it all, he might feel it had escaped him. 'What a falling off we make from nature', he said ruefully, looking at his first sketch of the two Calmady girls (cf no.41).

Inevitably, he sometimes faltered after initial enthusiasm. Not even he could always keep his artistic spirits excited under the steady pressure of demand. Yet the remarkable thing is not that he sometimes failed or grew tired but how frequently he succeeded. Competition, the opportunity for public display, the challenge implicit in the annual Royal Academy exhibitions provided exactly the right stimulus for him to concentrate all his gifts: to prepare and perfect the astonishing creatures of his illusionism to face the audience when eventually the curtain went up.

All his long working life he was required to perform in art, and he could have no doubt that, as with most performances, the dazzling feats concealed apprehension, lengthy difficulties and dogged labour. His career as a virtuoso had begun already at ten years old, fostered by the vanity of his egregious father (a father to hang in the dreadful gallery of artists' fathers beside Mozart's and Mengs's), when his pencil portraits were adroit though lacking much indication of his future. And his career ended fifty years later, with him at work on the day before his death: on, suitably, one more version of his full-length portrait of George IV (cf no.33), which he rallied himself from inertia to advance a little. In the studio were no less than fourteen replicas of this design alone, destined for places as far apart as Sierra Leone and New South Wales. Lawrence worked on the one to go to St Petersburg, dealing not with the face but, typically enough, with the detail of the left sleeve with its elaborate plumage of white satin ribbons and diamond studs. He denied it when his anxious, devoted friend Miss Croft asked if he was not tired of painting 'those eternal robes'; and to her he gave a final, significant comment on his art and its aims, explaining that while he preserved the same composition in all these royal portraits, he varied the details, so that he hoped if they were compared, 'you would find the last was still the best'.


Thomas Lawrence was born at Bristol on 13 April 1769. The year of his birth was also that of Napoleon and Wellington; such references not only serve as useful reminders of his generation and the world into which he grew up but have particular relevance for an artist who frequently painted Wellington (cf no.30) and seems to have felt a fascination with Napoleon, whose son he portrayed and whose second wife, Marie-Louise, was to entertain him at Parma.

Lawrence's father, also called Thomas, chose 1769 as the year to try being an inn-keeper, having previously tried being a supervisor of Excise. Ebullient, impractical and ultimately embarrassing, the elder Lawrence seems to have been a Mr Micawber of publicans. Soon failing with the White Lion at Bristol, he moved to the Black Bear at Devizes. There, in an inn conveniently situated, and already a popular stopping-place on the way to Bath, something turned up in the shape of the talent of his youngest son Tom, one of five surviving children. The boy was good-looking, quick to learn and fond of reciting poetry (all gifts to confirm his father in assuming the simplest laws of heredity). More truly unexpected and astonishing was his early manifested gift for drawing: for drawing people.

Although he could also copy pictures, it was inevitably his precocious ability to catch a likeness that attracted attention. That was an art which everyone might appreciate and many find useful; essentially it was a social talent, and the boy Lawrence grew up in, as it were, the society of his father's sometimes celebrated guests, displayed before them to display his gifts. His first biographer, Williams, rather well conveys how not every weary traveller reaching the Black Bear at evening welcomed the host's proffering of his son when food and a bed were looked for; but the boy survived – justified – even his father's eulogies. By the age of ten he could draw profiles such as those of the future Lord and Lady Kenyon (no.53a and b) – two people Williams names as having arrived at the inn tired, somewhat impatient and in no mood to appreciate an infant prodigy. Two years later 'Master Lawrence' was praised in print by Daines Barrington, brother of the Bishop of Durham (cf no.31), and someone whose interest in very youthful talent had led him, in the year of Lawrence's birth, to praise the boy Mozart.

According to Fanny Burney, an enthusiastic visitor in 1780, the inn was 'full of books, as well as paintings, drawings and music'. That was probably just as well, because Lawrence received little proper education; his love of literature and the theatre was instinctive rather than learned or perhaps very firmly based. For all his doubtless early acquired social polish and assurance, he remained culturally much less assured. The earliest pictorial image he himself recalled impressing him at Devizes when he was aged about four or five, was, significantly, a portrait; it was of Shakespeare, 'taken from the statue', and its pallor frightened him.

Nothing seems to have frightened Lawrence's father, whose pride in his talented son had in it a vein of shrewdness lacking in his handling of his own affairs. He became, or sought to become, the boy's impresario; and from early on it appears to have been accepted that the whole family should look to Lawrence's work to support them financially.

Lawrence was therefore taken from Devizes to be shown off, first at Oxford, where he drew portraits of more than fifty 'eminent personages', and then at Weymouth; finally the father followed in the steps of his own clients and went to Bath. The family had settled there before the end of 1780 and moved to London only after Lawrence's first appearance at the Royal Academy in 1787.

It was in Bath that the crucial first test of Lawrence's ability took place. He ceased to be a child there, and it must have been a question, briefly, if his precocity as an artist would also cease. Instead of portraits in pencil he now worked in pastel, producing small oval head-and-shoulders pictures – and he continued to charm and astonish. At Bath it became clear that his was not the short-lived freak gift of a boy but a talent of real potentiality, the more remarkable as its possessor was virtually self-taught.

Bath provided him with much more than opportunities for portraying fashionable visitors. It was in miniature the world, with its urban elegance, its society, theatres, collectors and art collections: at once Lawrence's school and his university, from which he passed effortlessly with the highest honours. He visited nearby great houses like Corsham. He was given the entrée to such old master collections as that formed by Mr Hamilton, the uncle of the Marquess of Abercorn (later his friend and patron; see no.22). Among the personalities he met and never forgot was Mrs Siddons (no.57); he drew his first portrait of her, and was years later to write a poem describing how to get a further sight of her he had run up the steep streets of Bath, 'just half pretending to be man'.

That phrase seems accidentally well illustrated by Lawrence's rapid sketch of himself aged about twelve (no.54), looking both exceptionally youthful and exceptionally poised and self-possessed. His appearance and his manner partly screened his personality but facilitated his easy passage into circles where famous and high-born figures would become friendly acquaintances, if not indeed friends, as well as sitters.

At Bath Lawrence started to paint a few pictures in oil, beginning in 1786 traditionally with a large-scale *Christ bearing the Cross*, presumably under the influence of old master pictures he had seen or knew through the medium of engraving. For a long while, perhaps secretly for most of his life, he aspired to be more than a painter of just portraits, but at the same time he recognized remarkably early – and with remarkable assurance – where his ability lay.

By, probably, the summer of 1787 he was in London with his father (who typically took lodgings in Leicester Square, surely because Sir Joshua Reynolds lived there). From London he wrote home to his mother, having by then met Reynolds and seen the work of Gainsborough and Romney. He told her he was painting a head of himself in oils, 'much approved of'; and he went on that though he would not say so outside the family, 'excepting Sir Joshua for the painting of a head, I would risk my reputation with any painter in London'.

Lawrence's ability as a pastellist was considerable, though in retrospect perhaps more competent than exciting. It can be fairly gauged from the *Elizabeth Carter* (no.56), exhibited at the Academy in 1790, which shows his grasp on character as much as likeness, and also his sympathetic response to the hint of vigorous 'no-nonsense' attitudes, unweakened by any physical frailty, in old ladies. It is sensed in this pastel and becomes patent as Lawrence speedily develops in the medium of oil his gallery of aged female sitters: from the Dowager Countess of Oxford (no.2), of about the same date, cheerfully beginning to grow like her pet dog, to domestically busy Lady Dundas (no.14), and culminating in the severe, semi-judicial scrutiny of Lady Robert Manners (no.46), thirty-six years later. Far more, incidentally, than the society beauties often associated with his art are these women heroines to Lawrence; he savours the matriarchal spell exuding from their big caps, wide hats and ruffs, all surrounding faces of uncompromising, time-tested individuality.

It was inevitable that with so much to express Lawrence should need more scope than was offered by the scale and medium of pastel. And in the same letter to his mother quoted above he tells her how when Prince Hoare (the son of the painter William Hoare whom he knew in Bath) saw his self-portrait in oils he realized he could not 'persuade me to go on in crayons'.

Lawrence exhibited a first full-length in oils, the portrait of Lady Cremorne (no.1), at the Academy in 1789. Of an oil he had shown in the previous year the *St James's Chronicle* had commented that, though it had merit, the artist should stick to pastel. And it seems that for a year or two the newspapers, and possibly the public, were uncertain how successful he would prove in oil paint.

The answer was given at the Academy exhibition of 1790, when Lawrence's highly varied group of a dozen pictures included the two full-length masterpieces of Queen Charlotte (no.3) and Miss Farren (no.4). Reynolds exhibited *Mrs Billington as S. Cecilia* (fig.2), one of his last portraits, at this, his last Academy. Contemporaries probably saw less the contrast between the President's singer 'ensky'd and sainted' and the new young painter's actress stepping as a private person through sunlit, proto-Constable countryside than the claim-cum-challenge to succeed Reynolds as *the* portrait painter which Lawrence's work represented. In the previous year one newspaper had called him 'the Sir Joshua of futurity'; and at the Academy of 1790 Reynolds himself paid Lawrence the measured compliment of saying: 'In you, sir, the world will expect to see accomplished all that I have failed to achieve'. Indeed, Lawrence had already achieved one thing not given to Reynolds for virtually a decade: sittings from the Queen.

The handling of paint in that portrait, as in *Miss Farren*, showed how little Lawrence was truly of Reynolds's school – or, in fact, of anyone's. His exuberant delight in juicy, unmuddy paint, laid on with almost sizzling freshness, was instinctive and his own; such lessons as he had had must have come from studying Rubens, Van Dyck, Rembrandt and ultimately Titian (in 1788 he was planning to copy 'a fine portrait' by Titian belonging to Lady Middleton). Yet the boldness he displayed was allied with sureness and uncanny accuracy of observation. At the very time he was orchestrating the massed and excitingly tactile effects of Queen Charlotte's lilac-grey crisp dress, with its gleaming, sorbet-like surface, the sweep of aquamarine curtain above her and the flashes of thick russet foliage in the landscape behind her, he could shift to the chamber-music idiom of chalks and produce the delicate, precise drawing of Mrs Papendiek and her son (no.55), turning her bonnet alone from a triumph of millinery into a triumph of linear art.

It is not just that Lawrence had been profoundly trained – self-trained – as a draughtsman and that he continued to draw expertly throughout his life. For him drawing was the method whereby he pinned down his prime visual sensations. 'La vérité de son dessin' was one of the qualities singled out by Delacroix, adding that his drawing of heads was 'incomparable'. In most cases it literally underlay his paintings. It was an apparatus, firm and rigid, which he constructed and on which he could perform those bravura feats of painting that first astonished the artistic world of London in 1790, as Miss Farren sprang up before them on the walls of the Academy, yet more sprightly than in life, bringing with her all the atmosphere of a summer's day, while no less vividly Queen Charlotte was created, seated somewhat brooding, as if on the passage of time, as autumn touched the trees at Windsor.

In the following year Lawrence's official success began with his election as an Associate of the Royal Academy. When Reynolds died in 1792 he was rapidly appointed in his place Painter-in-Ordinary to the King. In 1794, just before his twenty-fifth birthday, he was voted a full Academician – narrowly defeating Hoppner, aged about thirty-six, and thus doubtless whetting the edge of what soon became keen rivalry, lasting until Hoppner's death in 1810. At the Academy exhibition of 1794, which opened a few weeks after Lawrence's election, his friend Joseph Farington noted the general opinion 'that Lawrence this year is inferior to Hoppner'.

Apart from this annual and perhaps quite fruitful rivalry, Lawrence could feel himself established and little challenged by the mid 1790s. He was certainly the most sheerly exciting, as well as accomplished, portrait-painter in England; and among British painters of the period his closest rival in aesthetic terms is Raeburn, an artist who remained in Scotland, little otherwise known or patronized.

Very soon after settling in London Lawrence made –through his talents – the friends in whose families he became accepted as almost an honorary member: William Lock whom he painted and drew (no.66); John Julius Angerstein, for whom he painted one of his rare

FIG.2    Sir Joshua Reynolds, *Mrs Billington as S. Cecilia*, 1790. Gift of Lord Beaverbrook, Beaverbrook Art Gallery, Fredericton, N.B., Canada.

double full-lengths of husband and wife (no.7), an unusually sober image; the Boucheretts, whose daughter Emilia he sketched in an enchantingly tender and witty composition, gravely contemplating a doll as big as herself (no.59). These friends were affluent but not aristocratic, art-loving to some extent but very much amateurs, and not apparently very intellectual. It was probably a relief to Lawrence to be adopted by families where he need not talk about his art – need not perhaps talk at all; after his death Angerstein's son told Williams, 'his own opinions were not easily disclosed'.

Lawrence's parents both died in 1797, and Farington (twenty-two years his senior) became a sort of father to him: a more solid and satisfactory one than the elder Lawrence. On several occasions Lawrence referred to his own father; he believed he had inherited 'much of my father's carelessness', and as late as 1814 he lamented his parents' failure to secure for their son 'two or three parts in education of the utmost importance to the future happiness of the man'.

In the years leading up to 1800, and indeed beyond, Lawrence's life can be traced publicly through his paintings and privately through the drawings he continued to make chiefly for personal pleasure.

This was the period when he sometimes forced his art to a heroic pitch, and scale, which was true to his ambitions but not to his artistic imagination. His strong sense of the individual – alone, almost defiant against the world – gives its stormy Byronic glamour to *Lord Mountstuart* (no.10), who might be compared to a portrait by Goya. Yet at the same date – 1795 – he could depict a real hero and a man of action, Sir Charles Grey (no.11), with eighteenth-century ease and calm absence of panache. Colossal, fiendish pride was the mood he aimed at two years later in the large *Satan summoning his Legions* (Royal Academy), and it is still rumbling ominously – as well as more successfully – in the subsequent *Kemble as Coriolanus* (no.12), who towers against a background intended to be the hearth of Tullus Aufidius but remarkably like hell fire.

Privately, Lawrence might relax by drawing the odd caricature (no.60), the portrait of a friend like Fuseli (no.62) or the impression made on him by the moonlight over Sloane Street fields (no.64). But in these years his affairs – both financial and emotional – became desperately tangled and hopeless. Probably they did not harm his art – only sharpened it and increased his melancholy self-knowledge. He got into grave debt, for reasons not quite clear, and never fully got out of it, despite his large income. He fell in love with various women, notably the Siddons sisters Sally and Maria, and agonized a good deal accordingly. Yet it is hard to feel he was ever committed to marriage; an *amitié amoureuse* with Mrs Wolff and a warm if somewhat old-maidish friendship with Miss Croft (see no.80) seem to have come to satisfy him emotionally, while his art shows him profoundly touched – to a typical bachelor extent – by the appeal of mothers and children, of babies even, and of the family as such. Not defiance or pride, though maybe loneliness, can be detected in the poignant observation of certain drawings. Mr and Mrs Allnutt fondly rejoice over their infant daughter's existence (no.71). Amelia Lock tenderly cares for her valetudinarian father (no.66). And in perhaps the most intimate of all these drawings Mrs John Angerstein is seen nursing her child (no.74) with a directness of sympathy and handling that anticipates Renoir. Although Lawrence did not paint and exhibit pictures like this, much the same vein of feeling underlies famous and now underestimated portraits like those of Charles Lambton and the Calmady girls. His mothers care for, caress, or are caressed by, their children. Mrs Maguire seems really happy romping with her son (no.22), and if she, as a nobleman's mistress, is judged too disreputable to be typical, one might instance Mrs Henry Baring being played with and around by her high-spirited children (no.39).

These paintings carry Lawrence's career well into the next century and they reveal how he continued to invent challenges for himself, making his art evolve and deepen even while his outward life grew quieter, rather prosaic. He seems to have begun to understand that heroic, fanciful, semi-history pictures were not his *métier*. He had to find romance, history and heroism in the character of his contemporaries as they were. The challenge of Lord Thurlow, for example, lay in his very doggedness and toughness – his resolutely unglamorous appearance and personality. Lawrence responded with a wonderfully impressive, thoroughly tough yet not unsympathetic portrait (no.19), as apparently uncompromising as the sitter. It leads on to the ambitious group of the Barings (no.23), a great success at the Academy of 1807, which might be dubbed Lawrence's re-doing of Rembrandt's *Staalmeesters*. Banking is given its own glamour and even drama, with Charles Wall turning the pages of a vast ledger and John Baring crouched tensely at the table, while Sir Francis Baring – deaf yet dominant in the composition as in life – strains to hear.

Part of the complex genius of Lawrence lay in the variety of his responses. By the early 1800s he had channelled and refined his early exuberance. He now managed paint with greater subtlety but no less affection. Overwhelmed he might be with commissions; still his flair did not fail him. He could portray Thurlow, as also many another characterful old man (and woman), with a plain, blunt manner that seems to extend from composition to actual handling of the medium. On the other hand, nothing could be more complicated than the composition of *Mrs Maguire and her son* (no.22), painted in the period between *Thurlow* and the Baring group. And nothing could better convey melting, almost bacchic indolence after the restraints of the law and high finance: boy, dog and mother all sprawled on the floor, and all a little askew in their circular framing as if slightly tipsy amid the clusters of grapes.

Around 1810 martial glamour, stirring events, and a new, most significant friendship entered Lawrence's life in the person of Sir Charles Stewart, Castlereagh's half-brother and Wellington's adjutant-general. He was to sit for more than one portrait, but the familiar image (no.28) seems to express a generation as well as a man: the *homme fatal* as conceived contemporaneously in France by painters like Gros. It was fortunate that an engraving of Lawrence's portrait, catching all its brilliance and swagger, should have been published in 1814, the year of Allied victory over Napoleon; it was sent to the Prince Regent and certainly played its part in his commissioning Lawrence to paint portraits of the visiting monarchs of Russia (no.35) and Prussia and their generals Platov and Blücher. That was the germ of the Waterloo Chamber series of sovereigns and statesmen involved in Napoleon's overthrow. Personally too Stewart helped Lawrence by commissioning from him at the same period a portrait of the Regent; and it was Stewart who presented the painter to the Prince at a levee on 28 July 1814. Lawrence later looked back gratefully to Stewart as involved in, if not initiating, the process 'which led to all subsequent distinctions in my profession'.

During Hoppner's lifetime the Prince had patronized him a good deal, and only now did he effectively 'discover' Lawrence. His patronage of him for virtually the rest of their lives (he survived Lawrence by only six months) was as near creative as patronage can ever be. It gave the artist impetus and the tremendous opportunities which led to such portraits as the *Archduke Charles* (no.37), painted in Vienna in 1819, and *Pope Pius VII* (no.38), painted at Rome a few months later. The Archduke, who was physically small, looms tall and still against a stormy atmospheric sky (suggestive of serious study of Turner), convincingly a commander without swagger or heroics; he is Lawrence's mature expression of the mood aimed at in such a portrait as *Kemble as Coriolanus*, of some twenty years before. Life at last is matching the artist's dreams; and it culminated by bringing him, the English heir of Raphael and Titian and Velazquez, to paint the

FIG.3    *George IV*, 1822. By courtesy of the
Wallace Collection: Crown Copyright.

FIG.4    *Lady Peel*, 1827. Copyright the Frick Collection, New York.

successor of St Peter, the Supreme Pontiff, who proved also good, kind and lively even in extreme old age. The Holy Father was perhaps what Lawrence had always been seeking.

For the purpose of his European mission the Regent had knighted Lawrence in 1815, just a month or two before the battle of Waterloo. His mission was delayed, and meanwhile the Regent sat for the most memorably glamorous of all Lawrence's male portraits, that of himself in Garter robes (no.33). In January 1820 he ascended the throne as George IV, and shortly afterwards Lawrence returned from the Continent to be elected President of the Royal Academy.

Lawrence had a decade left of life and activity. The confidence he had gained by working abroad is seen in the steady stream of masterpieces – varied in scale and varied in sitter – that he produced for each year's Academy exhibition. One fine portrait not exhibited there was his full-length of the King (fig.3), seen in private dress and aspect, no longer posing in uniform or robes but looking very much at gentlemanly ease, dignified without any insistence upon rank. The showy earlier image might go on being required officially for palaces and embassies, but this quieter one has greater conviction. It accords with Lawrence's late and level penetrating scrutiny which, while never disturbing a sitter's composure, seems earnestly concerned to convey character. In addition to the great portraits of children, he portrayed as impressively the bald Duke of Bedford (no.40) and the monkey-like Nash (no.47) as the slightly fading spinster Princess Sophia (no.43) or the opulent beauty of Lady Peel (fig.4), where despite her bird of paradise plumes, expanse of fur and heavy bracelets like jewelled manacles the sitter gazes out with simplicity and sweetness.

To appreciate Lawrence's range and mastery during the last decade, this portrait (of 1827) should mentally be added, along with the George IV, to what is included in the present exhibition. Its combination of qualities can indeed hardly be duplicated and may partly be explained by Lawrence's acquaintance with the sitter, the wife of the man who had become the greatest of his non-royal patrons, and also by the fact that the portrait was vaguely intended as a pendant to Rubens's *Chapeau de Paille*, which Peel owned. Lawrence was thus brought into direct association with an old master painting (one by the painter whose work he had first admired as a child at Bath, visiting Corsham), and implicitly challenged to rival art as well as nature. A further bond between him and Peel must have been that they were both collectors; and though Peel could afford to buy paintings far beyond Lawrence's resources, Lawrence's ever-increasing collection of magnificent old master drawings – one reason doubtless for his chronic debts – was unrivalled.

Lawrence died suddenly on 7 January 1830, leaving society and the public stunned by the unexpected news. In fact he had for some time felt a dwindling of vitality and a sense of mortal chill, though he fought against it. On Boxing Day 1829 he had written: 'I am chained to the oar; but painting was never less inviting to me – business never more oppressive . . .' He struggled and rallied: dined for the last time at Peel's house (Peel gave him a fresh commission, for a self-portrait) and forced himself back to art, the nourishment which had never failed him in his career of over fifty years. He put brush very briefly to one of those fourteen versions of George IV's portrait; he gazed wistfully at a portfolio of prints after a drawing of his, and when eventually he was too weak for anything else, he lay listening to an article read aloud by his imminent executor on the genius of Flaxman. Less than half an hour later he was dead.

A more than normally splendid funeral was arranged for Lawrence, of more than normally sterile effect. Three earls were among the pall-bearers, as well as Peel. It became a public pageant. To *The Times*, reporting it on 21 January 1830, it was remarkable because 'Byron's funeral did not excite nearly so much public attention'. A concourse of carriages had followed the mourners to St Paul's, but the carriages were empty; most of Lawrence's high-born acquaintances did not bother to attend, and it was noted that the royal family was quite unrepresented.

Lawrence died as he had lived, deeply in debt. His superb old master drawings were refused by both the King and the nation at the bargain price stipulated in his will, and tragically dispersed. His bequests were void; everything he owned had to be sold. When in 1832 Benjamin Robert Haydon visited his big house at 65 Russell Square it was dirty and desolate: 'He occupied a parlour and a bedroom; all the rest of the house was turned to business'. That might serve as a summing-up of Lawrence's existence, given over from his earliest years to the business of being an artist. Nothing at the end was left except his art; and that remains.

# Some of Lawrence's Views and Opinions

Fig.5    *Self-portrait, c.1825* (unfinished).
By courtesy of the Royal Academy of Arts, London.

To any but my own family I certainly should not say *this*; but, excepting Sir Joshua, for the painting of a head, I would risk my reputation with any painter in London.
*1787 or 1788*

I should think it always better that the picture, whatever it is, be first accurately drawn on the canvas . . .
*1790*

I have found much benefit from the severest criticism.
*1794*

I am myself unalterably convinc'd of the advantage of making colour'd sketches from Nature . . .
*1810*

[I] am as much the slave of the picture I am painting as if it had living, personal existence, and had chained me to it.
*c.1810*

'Tis hard to toil and struggle for some subtle refinement of a Tone or harmony of Lines that shall unite a whole, where the *Parts* have been of arduous execution, in order to meet the prompt decision of one rapid glance of Ignorance!
*1815*

[In your own line of art do you consider (the Elgin marbles) of high importance, as forming a national school?]
In a line of art which I have very seldom practised, but which it is still my wish to do so, I consider that they would; viz. historical painting.
*1816*

Sir Thomas Lawrence is sorry that he must decline to obey His Lordship's wishes in sending the Pictures, as he cannot consent that his Works should be finish'd by other Artists . . .
*1818*

. . . but certainly I have less and less confidence as I grow old . . . You know how long it is before one gets under weigh [sic] in Painting – before the Pencil can mould the Color into shape, before that shape has *general* accuracy of form . . .
*1818*

Even the amount of my labours [on the Continent], considering all things, is not little; and when the subjects of them are remembered, and the NERVOUS DIFFICULTIES OF THE TASK, and that I have in no instance failed in it . . .
*1819*

I exist more and more in the love of art.
*1823*

The salutary effects of yearly competition, and its advancing knowledge, are indeed incalculable.
*1826*

For me, to use your dear father's expression [J. J. Angerstein], I shall live and die in harness.
*1829*

# Catalogue Notes

Both paintings and drawings are catalogued in approximate chronological order. Measurements are given in centimetres, followed by inches in brackets, height before width.

The following abbreviations have been used:

| | |
|---|---|
| Garlick, 1954 | Kenneth Garlick, *Sir Thomas Lawrence*, 1954 |
| Garlick, 1964 | Kenneth Garlick, *A catalogue of the paintings, drawings and pastels of Sir Thomas Lawrence* (Walpole Society, Vol.XXXIX, 1962–4), 1964 |
| Layard | George Soames Layard, *Sir Thomas Lawrence's Letter-Bag*, 1906 |
| Millar | Oliver Millar, *Later Georgian Pictures in the Collection of Her Majesty The Queen*, 1969 |
| R.A. | Royal Academy |
| Williams | D. E. Williams, *Life and Correspondence of Sir Thomas Lawrence, Kt.*, 1831 (2 vols) |

The literature pre–Garlick, 1964, including references to exhibitions, has been cited in the entries only when it has particular relevance for the discussion; it will be found fully listed by Garlick. Note has usually been taken here of post 1964 exhibitions, but no claim is made that this is exhaustive.

References to the *Diary* kept by Joseph Farington, RA, from 1793 to 1821, are from the typescript deposited in the British Museum of the original manuscript in the Royal Library, Windsor, except where volumes of the complete text of the *Diary* being edited by K. Garlick and A. Macintyre have been published; page references are given to this edition. Permission to quote from the *Diary* has graciously been granted by Her Majesty the Queen.

A biography of Lawrence, concentrating almost entirely on his life and not attempting to discuss his art, is *Regency Portrait Painter* by Douglas Goldring, 1951.

# Paintings

## 1 Viscountess Cremorne (c.1740–1826)

Canvas, 241.2 × 144.8 (95 × 57)
*Provenance*: From the collection of the Earl of
Dartrey.
*Literature*: Garlick, 1954, p.33; 1964, p.61.

Philadelphia Hannah, daughter of Thomas Freame of
Philadelphia, and granddaughter of William Penn,
married Thomas, 1st and only Viscount Cremorne
(1725–1813), as his second wife in 1770. Her age is
given as eighty-six at the time of her death (*Gentleman's
Magazine*, 14 April 1826). She wears what must be a
form of Quaker dress.

Exhibited by Lawrence at the Royal Academy in
1789 (no.100). He also painted a full-length companion
portrait of Lord Cremorne about the same date. Both
pictures must be among Lawrence's earliest portraits in
oils. The head in the present picture has been claimed
by C. Merrill Mount (cf Garlick, 1964) as based on a
portrait of the sitter by Gilbert Stuart. This would be
altogether unusual, and certainly the head here seems
not based on the Stuart portrait of Lady Cremorne
reproduced in the *Connoisseur*, April 1937, p.215,
where the cap, for example, worn by the sitter is
different.

According to the *World*, 20 October 1789: 'It is
Lady Cremorne's portrait and Lord Mulgrave's that
introduced Mr Lawrence to the Queen' (cf no.3). In
reviews of the 1789 exhibition other newspapers, while
generally praising Lawrence's work, said little of the
present picture, with the exception of the *St James's
Chronicle*, 2–5 May: 'A good resemblance . . . The
background is well conceived and finely painted. The
figure wants ease and grace'.

In a list of Lawrence's portraits 'painted prior to, or
immediately after' his coming to London (Williams, I,
p.127) the present picture is priced at forty guineas.

*Private collection*

Not available for exhibition.

2

## 2   Susanna, Countess of Oxford (1728-1804)

Canvas, 125.8 × 99.7 (49½ × 39¼)
*Provenance*: By descent in the family of the sitter's
husband; bought by the 2nd Lord Bateman and
afterwards acquired for the Fyvie Castle collection.
*Literature*: Garlick, 1954, p.53; 1964, p.156.

Susanna, daughter of William Archer of Welford,
Berkshire, married Edward, 4th Earl of Oxford (1726-
90), in 1751. There were no children of the marriage.
At the sitter's death the *Gentleman's Magazine*
(November 1804) recorded of her: 'To the poor she
was a liberal benefactress, and her death will long be
regretted by everyone who knew her.'
   The picture is a companion to one of the Earl in the
same collection. Garlick dates the pair to around 1789,
but the confident, bravura handling of the present
picture seems markedly in advance of *Lady Cremorne*
(no.1), and it need not have been finished at the time
of the 4th Earl's death in 1790. There seems no mention
of the pictures among contemporary references to
Lawrence's early work.

*Sir Andrew G. Forbes-Leith, Bt*

## 3   Queen Charlotte (1744-1818)

Canvas, 239.4 × 147.3 (94¼ × 58)
*Provenance*: In Lawrence's possession until his death;
bought by Sir Matthew White Ridley at the
Lawrence sale, 18 June 1831 (lot 133), and in Ridley
family possession until bought by the National
Gallery, 1927.
*Literature*: Garlick, 1954, p.32; Garlick, 1964, p.54;
M. Levey, *A Royal Subject, Portraits of Queen
Charlotte*, 1977.

Sophie Charlotte of Mecklenburg-Strelitz married
George III in 1761. She is shown wearing bracelets
with a portrait miniature of the King and his cipher.
   Exhibited at the Academy in 1790 (no.100) and,
along with the full-length portrait of Miss Farren (no.4
here), helped to make Lawrence's name as the most
gifted portrait-painter of the young generation and as
the successor, if not rival, of Reynolds. It was his first
major royal commission, though it was not acquired
by the King or Queen.
   The instigation for its commissioning is not clear,
but there is a mention of it, not previously remarked,
amid praise of Lawrence which appeared in the *World*
as early as 17 July 1789, listing his portraits 'yet to
come' including one of the Queen. Lawrence was
summoned to Windsor at the Queen's command on
27 September 1789, with a view to her sitting on the
following day. She chose the dress to be painted in;
Lawrence disliked the bonnet and hat she proposed
wearing, and she decided to be painted bare-headed (an
effect which upset George III when he saw the picture).
In a desire for her features to look animated Lawrence
proposed she should talk; the Queen thought this
'rather presuming', and eventually she refused him
further sittings. The Assistant Keeper of her Wardrobe,
Mrs Papendick (cf no.55), was finally allowed to sit for
such details as the bracelets. Her memoirs give the
circumstances stated above (*Court and Private Life in the
time of Queen Charlotte*, ed. Mrs V. Delves Broughton,
1887, II, pp.133-4 and 141-3).
   The Queen had been, and was to be, successfully
portrayed by several painters, notably Gainsborough,
who had died in 1788. When a fresh full-length
portrait of her was under consideration the next year,
Gainsborough's death and the growing fame of a
talented new artist may have combined, with royal
dislike of Reynolds, in the choice of Lawrence. But the
outbreak of the King's illness in 1788 had shocked and
aged the Queen; and in the summer of 1789 she was
further shocked by the outbreak of the French
Revolution. Although the resulting image was
praised, outside the royal family, and admired as a
likeness, it somehow failed to please. X-rays show that

3

in the final portrait the painter modified somewhat the Queen's grim, careworn expression he first observed. The 1790 exhibition included a portrait of Queen Charlotte by Russell which the *St James's Chronicle* thought not a good resemblance: 'the mouth has not the peculiar character of the original'.

Reviews of the exhibition warmly praised Lawrence's picture: 'A strong resemblance . . . the whole extremely well finished; and the landscape in the background very beautiful' (*St James's Chronicle*), and mentioned it among the best work on show. Lawrence's father wrote a letter of 30 April 1790 (Douglas Goldring, *Regency Portrait Painter*, 1951, pp.

86-7) conveniently assembling several other reviews, including that of the *World*, '. . . certainly a performance of which Vandyke himself would have been proud', and the *Gazetteer*, 'a most perfect likeness'. The *Morning Chronicle* thought the portrait 'admirable in point of likeness . . . but the landscape will merit of improvement'.

A letter of 25 November 1816 from Lawrence to Farington refers to painting a portrait of the Queen (R.A., MSS Law/2/167), perhaps related to the sketch in his posthumous sale, 18 June 1831 (lot 13).

*The Trustees of the National Gallery*

## 4 Elizabeth Farren, later Countess of Derby (c.1759–1829)

*Colour plate I, page 33.*

4

Canvas, 238.8 × 146.1 (94 × 57½)
*Provenance*: From the 12th Earl of Derby's collection, passed to the sitter's daughter who married the 2nd Earl of Wilton; acquired from the collection of the 4th Earl (d.1898) or the 5th Earl of Wilton by Ludwig Neumann, by 1904; J. Pierpont Morgan by 1906; Edward S. Harkness in or c.1935.
*Literature*: Garlick, 1954, p.37; 1964, p.79; *Masterpieces of Fifty Centuries*, Metropolitan Museum of Art, New York, 1970 (no.339).

Elizabeth Farren appeared first as an actress in London at the Haymarket theatre in 1777. She married the 12th Earl of Derby, as his second wife, in 1797 and retired from the stage. Portraits of her by numerous other artists include a full-length as Hermione in *The Winter's Tale* by Zoffany, c.1780, and a half-length drawing by Downman of 1787. Hazlitt in his *Essays on the Drama* (1820) referred to her 'fine-lady airs and graces, with that elegant turn of the head . . .'

Exhibited at the Academy in 1790 (no.171), when it was by a slip catalogued simply as of 'An Actress'. Lawrence's long letter of apology to Miss Farren exists in draft (Layard, pp.12–13); in this he explains that he intended it to be catalogued as a portrait of a lady, 'and this he did as well from its being Miss Farren in Private as from the wish he had that it should be known to be her from the likeness alone, unaided by professional character'.

These phrases help to underline the direct, natural and almost *plein-air* approach of the portrait (dispensing with the stock properties of curtains and plinths) which makes greater the contrast with Reynolds's allegorical *Mrs Billington as S. Cecilia* (fig.2), exhibited in the same year.

Two undated letters from Miss Farren to Lawrence (Layard, pp.14–15) record that Lord Derby 'meant to be the purchaser' and that her appearance in the picture had been criticized as 'so thin in the figure, that you might blow it away . . . you must make it a little *fatter*, at all events, diminish the *bend* you are so attached to . . .'

The original price of the picture was set at sixty guineas, but after other potential purchasers had offered him a hundred, Lawrence raised the price accordingly. Miss Farren's astonished reaction is given in a letter (Layard, p.14). Mrs Papendiek (op. cit. under no.3, II, p.199) also records Lawrence's raising of the price.

Understandably, the picture was very well received, at least one newspaper comparing it with Reynolds's *Mrs Billington* to the latter's disadvantage: 'in spirit, colouring and expression far superior' (*English Chronicle*, 29 April–1 May). The *St James's Chronicle*, 4 May, said: 'A most spirited resemblance . . . The figure is easy and natural, the affectation of the original is well disguised. The sattin [sic] cloak and fur are admirably painted . . .' The *Public Advertiser*, 30 April, was even more enthusiastic and percipient: '. . . might create envy in the mind of the first artist that ever existed. We have seen a great variety of pictures of Miss Farren, but we never before saw her mind and character upon canvas. It is completely Elizabeth Farren; arch, spirited, elegant and engaging'. The same sentences had appeared in the *Diary*, quoted by Lawrence's father in the letter cited under no.3 above, including 'careless' among the adjectives describing Miss Farren.

*Metropolitan Museum of Art, New York
(Bequest of Edward S. Harkness, 1940)*

**5    Georgina, Lady Apsley, later Countess
Bathurst (1765–1841)**

Canvas, 74.9 × 62.2 ($29\frac{1}{2}$ × $24\frac{1}{2}$)
*Provenance*: By family descent.
*Literature*: Garlick, 1954, p.25; 1964, p.30.

Georgina, third daughter of Lord George Lennox,
MP, married Henry, Lord Apsley (later 3rd Earl
Bathurst) in 1789.

All three daughters of Lord George Lennox
apparently sat to Lawrence around 1789, and from the
first there seems to have been some confusion as to the
identity of the portraits of them exhibited by
Lawrence. The present picture appears certainly to be

that shown at the Academy in 1792 (no.150) as a lady of
quality. A copy of the R.A. catalogue in the National
Gallery Library is annotated under no.150, 'L$^y$ Apsley'.
Another portrait, 'A Lady of Quality', no.232 in the
exhibition of 1789, was identified in some newspapers
as of Lady Apsley but this report was corrected in the
*Morning Herald* of 25 May that year: '. . . erroneously
applied to Lady Apsley; it is however more like the
lady for whom it was done, namely, her sister Miss
Lennox. Lady Apsley is now sitting to Mr Lawrence,
and Mrs Berkeley is to follow.'

In reviewing the 1792 exhibition *The Times* of 10

May repeated the exact words of praise of this portrait which had appeared in the *St James's Chronicle* of 1–3 May: 'The colouring of the head beautiful and chaste; and the stile of the background rich and simple. The whole forms a charming picture.' The *Public Advertiser*, 1 May, noted approvingly that Lawrence's paintings 'have now more solidity and less glitter than they had', and may have been referring specifically to this work.

In the list of Lawrence's portraits 'painted prior to, or immediately after' his coming to London (Williams, I, p.127) the present picture is priced at twenty guineas.

*The Earl Bathurst*

## 6   Arthur Atherley (1772–1844)

Canvas, 125.8 × 100.4 (49½ × 39½)
*Provenance*: With Mrs Killett and Mrs Pesne, London, by descent; William Randolph Hearst, 1928; Marion Davies, from whom bought and presented to the Los Angeles County Museum of Art, 1947.
*Literature*: Garlick, 1954, p.25; 1964, p.24; *Romantic Art in Britain*, Detroit and Philadelphia, 1968 (no.104); R.A., *Bicentenary Exhibition*, London, 1968–9 (no.185).

Arthur Atherley, elder son of Arthur Atherley of Southampton. Educated at Eton (see below), 1787–91. A banker in the firm of Atherley and Fall; MP for Southampton, 1806–7, 1812–18, 1831–3. An obituary in the *Gentleman's Magazine* (July–December 1844, p.650) gives his age at death as seventy-four but his death certificate states his age as seventy-two, and he was admitted a pensioner at Trinity College, Cambridge, 6 May 1790, then aged eighteen.

Exhibited at the Academy in 1792 (no.209) as 'Portrait of an Etonian', and probably commissioned in 1791 when Atherley was leaving Eton (seen in the distance right). It is mentioned by Williams (I, p.128) among Lawrence's work of 'about 1792, 1793, etc.' with its price as fifty guineas.

The picture was favourably noticed by the *St James's Chronicle* (1–3 May) and by *The Times* (10 May) in exactly the same words: 'A rich and spirited head; the background in the manner of Rembrandt. – Eton College is well introduced.' The *Morning Herald* (3 May) declared: 'This picture might be placed by the side of the best of Sir Joshua's, and the Artist would be entitled to exclaim with the conscious pride of Corregio [sic] . . . I too am a painter.'

Garlick, 1964, loc. cit., records an unfinished head of the sitter, with a blue coat, in the collection of Colonel H. D. M. Crichton-Maitland.

*Los Angeles County Museum of Art*
*(William Randolph Hearst Collection)*

6

## 7   Mr and Mrs John Julius Angerstein

Canvas, 254 × 158 (100 × 62⅜)
*Provenance*: In family possession until *c*.1896 when sold; acquired in that year by the Louvre.
*Literature*: Garlick, 1954, p.24; 1964, pp.18–19.

John Julius Angerstein (1735–1823), merchant and art collector, was one of Lawrence's earliest patrons and among his closest friends. He sat to Lawrence for several later portraits. At Lawrence's instigation his collection was sold to the Government after his death and became the nucleus of the National Gallery.

Angerstein's first wife died in 1783. In 1785 he married Eliza Lucas, née Payne, widow of Thomas Lucas; she died in 1800, aged fifty-one.

Exhibited at the Academy in 1792 (no.25) as of 'a gentleman and his lady'. The distant glimpse right of the sea and a sailing ship seems to hint at Angerstein's mercantile interests. Some later references (eg Garlick, 1954 and 1964, loc. cit.) erroneously describe the woman as Angerstein's first wife.

What are two presumably smaller and earlier portraits of Mr and Mrs Angerstein are referred to publicly as early as 1789 (the *World*, 17 July of that year), among work already executed. Conceivably, the heads in the present picture are based on these. It seems to have attracted little or no newspaper comment at the 1792 exhibition.

A repetition of the figure of Mrs Angerstein only is recorded by Garlick, 1964, loc. cit.

*Musée du Louvre*

7    *Mr and Mrs John Julius Angerstein*

8

## 8  Lady Charlotte Greville (1775–1862)

Canvas, 76.2 × 63.1 (30 × 24⅞)
*Provenance*: Presented by the 3rd Duke of Portland
(d.1809) to the future 6th Duke of Devonshire.
*Literature*: Garlick, 1954, p.27; 1964, pp.94–5.

Lady Charlotte Bentinck, elder daughter of the 3rd
Duke of Portland, married Charles, son of Fulke
Greville, in 1792. She became a close friend of the
Duke of Wellington. Among her children was the
diarist Charles Greville. A later portrait of her by
Lawrence is at Goodwood. Her father sat to Lawrence
for a full-length portrait commissioned *c*.1790
(Corporation of Bristol).

Exhibited at the Academy in 1792 (no.225) and
presumably painted for the sitter's father, some of
whose other children also sat a few years later to
Lawrence (pictures at Welbeck).

In the list of 'portraits painted . . . about the years
1792, 1793, etc.' (Williams, I, p.128), priced at twenty-
five guineas.

*The Trustees of the Chatsworth Settlement*

9

## 9  Emma, Lady Hamilton (1761?–1815)

Canvas, 243.8 × 152.4 (96 × 60)
*Provenance*: By family descent.
*Literature*: Garlick 1954, p.41; 1964, p.99.

Emma Hart married Sir William Hamilton in 1791;
she was later the mistress of Nelson. She was noted for
her beauty and was a favourite subject with painters,
notably Romney, who was painting her by 1786.

Exhibited at the Academy in 1792 (no.1) as of 'a lady
of fashion as La Penserosa'. The classical dancing figure
on the bas relief adjoining the sitter may allude to her
admired 'attitudes' and also to Hamilton's collection of
antiques.

In 1790 Lawrence had written to his friend Samuel
Lysons about the prospect of being introduced 'at Sir
William Hamilton's, to see this wonderful woman you
have doubtless heard of – Mrs Hart . . . I hear it is the
most gratifying thing to a painter's eye that can be'
(Williams, I, p.103). In an undated letter (R.A., MSS

Law/1/79) to an unknown correspondent he criticized Romney's depictions of her as more showing 'the artist's feebleness than her Grandeur'. A profile drawing of her by Lawrence (British Museum) is dated (not by the artist) 1791 and is loosely allied to her appearance in the present painting, though less idealized.

According to the *Morning Herald* (3 May 1792) the picture successfully combined the individual likeness with the character of Milton's 'Pensive Nun', and it mildly misquoted from *Il Penseroso* (ll.39-40):

Her looks commercing with the skies,
Her rapt soul sitting in her eyes.

Other newspapers were less favourable in their comments. The *Public Advertiser* (1 May) thought all Lawrence's portraits exhibited that year (eg nos.5, 6, 7 and 8 here) were successful with the exception of this. The *World* (4 May) said the painter had not done justice to the sitter's 'perfect symmetry of figure' and her reputation for 'disposing it in the most beautiful and captivating attitudes . . . the general effect is displeasing'. However, the *St James's Chronicle* (1-3 May), followed word for word by *The Times* (10 May), found 'some sublimity in the conception . . . The head is expressive; the figure grand . . .'

Two other smaller portraits of the sitter by Lawrence are recorded by Garlick, 1964, p.99.

*The Duke of Abercorn*

10

## 10  John, Lord Mountstuart (1767–94)
*Colour plate II, page 36*

Canvas, 238.8 × 147.3 (94 × 58)
*Provenance*: By family descent.
*Literature*: Garlick 1954, p.51; 1964, p.146.

Lord Mountstuart, eldest son of the Marquess of Bute; MP for Cardiff. He died as a result of a fall from his horse. An obituary in the *Gentleman's Magazine*, 20 January 1794, said: '. . . his heart glowed with the virtues which were rendered irresistibly endearing by the brilliancy of his accomplishments'. He had travelled in Spain and is shown wearing Spanish costume; a view of the Escorial in the background at the left.

Exhibited at the Academy in 1795 (no.86). There seems no reason for a supposition that the background with the Escorial was painted by Owen. The *True Briton* (13 May 1795) gave a long notice to the picture,

saying that for the background the artist was indebted 'to a well-known landscape by Rubens'. Some versions of a composition based on a drawing of the Escorial by Rubens were in English private collections (notably that of the Earl of Radnor). On 4 March 1796 Farington (*Diary*, ed. K. Garlick and A. Macintyre, II, 1978, p.503) noted a picture of 'the Escorial by Rubens' as having been sent to Christie's. The same newspaper thought the picture good but stigmatized 'the hideous cap' which the sitter had chosen to wear. The *Morning Post* spoke of 'eccentricities of the pencil at which delicacy must blush, and modesty turn aside'. Farington records (5 May 1795, *Diary*, op. cit. II, 1978, p.339) that Hoppner told him that the King, visiting the exhibition a few days previously, 'started back with disgust' on seeing the present portrait. The *St James's Chronicle* found the figure 'well drawn' and the scenery 'grand', but thought 'the whole wants brilliancy'.

Garlick, 1964, p.146, records a half-length version twice exhibited during the nineteenth century.

*Private collection*

COLOUR PLATE I   *Elizabeth Farren, later Countess of Derby* (no.4)

## 11 Sir Charles Grey, later 1st Earl Grey (1729-1807)

Canvas, 124.5 × 99.1 (49 × 39)
*Provenance*: By family descent.
*Literature*: Garlick, 1954, p.40; 1964, p.95.

Sir Charles Grey, a distinguished soldier; wounded in the battles of Minden and Campen, 1759, 1760; KB, 1782. Cooperated with Vice-Admiral Jervis in the capture of the French West Indies, 1794. Made general and privy councillor, 1795; created earl, 1806. He wears the star of the Order of the Bath.

Exhibited at the Academy in 1795 (no.131). The fortress flying the Union Jack in the background left must be meant for that of Martinique, gained in 1794. There seem to be conscious echoes in the composition of Reynolds's portrait of *Lord Heathfield* (National Gallery), which Lawrence admired and later owned.

The portrait was praised in the *True Briton* (13 May) as 'a spirited likeness', though the background was criticized as being too full of smoke. The *St James's Chronicle* thought the picture 'A good resemblance . . . We think it one of Lawrence's best works'.

Grey's son, later 2nd Earl, was painted by Lawrence on three occasions (R.A., 1793 (no.614); 1805 (no.96) and 1828 (no.158)); and cf no.87 here. He wrote on 10 January 1830 to Princess Lieven at Lawrence's death: 'He is a great loss to the art, and I regret him personally' (*Correspondence of Princess Lieven and Earl Grey*, ed. G. Le Strange, 1890, I, p.408).

*Private collection*

## 12 John Philip Kemble as Coriolanus

Canvas, 261.2 × 177.8 (113 × 70)
*Provenance*: Bought from Lawrence by Sir Richard Worsley; presented by the Earl of Yarborough to the Guildhall, 1906.
*Literature*: Garlick, 1954, p.44; 1964, p.115.

John Philip Kemble (1757-1823), actor and son of the actor Roger Kemble, whose other actor children included Mrs Siddons (cf no.57). At Drury Lane from 1783 to 1802 he appeared as Hamlet and in *King John*, *Othello*, *King Lear*, etc. One of his great parts was Coriolanus; he first played it, in his own adaptation of Shakespeare's play, in 1789, and took farewell of the stage in the part in 1817.

Exhibited at the Academy in 1798 (no.225): 'Mr Kemble as Coriolanus at the hearth of Tullus Aufidius'. In *Coriolanus*, Act IV, scene V, the recently banished Roman hero waits disguised in the house of the Volscian enemy Tullus Aufidius, having decided in anger to join with him against Rome.

Lawrence was friendly with Kemble and painted him several times; he showed a portrait of him at the Academy first in 1797. He had known the Kemble family since his boyhood days in Bath. At Kemble's death his widow replied to Lawrence's condolences with a letter expressing the actor's admiration of 'your extraordinary talents' and saying he felt a pride in 'having a conviction that by your aid he should be remembered'.

As late as 1811 Lawrence was inviting Farington to go with him to see Kemble in *Coriolanus*, writing 'I have seen it but once' (Layard, p.86).

In painting the picture, Lawrence thought of it as more than a portrait. An undated letter of *c*.1797 to Mrs Boucherett (Williams, I, p.197) refers to it as 'nearly finished', and he terms it, significantly, 'a sort of half-history picture'. In 1797 Lawrence had exhibited his large-scale, ambitious picture of *Satan summoning his legions*, which was generally accounted a failure. Not only the scale of the *Kemble as Coriolanus*, and the dominant central figure, but the choice of moment depicted – an act of rebellious pride by a banished leader – seem to echo the *Satan*, suggesting that Lawrence was now seeking a way to combine his known ability with his aspirations.

Farington noted (*Diary*, 9 January 1798) that Lawrence was working on the picture, and on 10 February he recorded that Dance liked the portrait. The newspapers received it very warmly, though several commented unfavourably on its greenish tone. The *Monthly Mirror* (May 1798) welcomed Lawrence's continued presentation of 'specimens in which the historical energy is predominant'. The *True Briton* (24

12    *John Philip Kemble as Coriolanus*

Colour Plate II  *John, Lord Mountstuart* (no.10)

COLOUR PLATE III   *Lady Elizabeth Foster, later Duchess of Devonshire* (no.21)

April) thought it painted 'with a powerful hand . . . suitable to the elevated character of historical portrait'. The *St James's Chronicle* (24-26 April) found in it 'an union of the style of Titian with that of Rembrandt'. 'One of his finest pictures', said the *Whitehall Evening Post* (21-24 April). The *Oracle* (24 April) called it 'very sublime and impressive'. The *Morning Chronicle* (23 April) thought it 'very grand'.

Kemble was also painted as Coriolanus by Bourgeois. On 13 September 1804 Farington (*Diary*) noted that Kemble had given that portrait to Boaden, the journalist and playwright, and put up in his drawing-room over the fireplace the present picture.

A sketch for the picture was in the Lawrence sale, 15 May 1830 (lot 20).

*Guildhall Art Gallery*

## 13 John Allnutt (c.1774-1863)

Canvas, 238.8 × 147.3 (94 × 58)
*Provenance*: By family descent.
*Literature*: Garlick, 1954, p.24; 1964, p.17.

The sitter was a wine merchant, a collector and a considerable patron of British artists, including Constable as well as Lawrence (cf also no.71). He lived at Clapham Common. He died on 12 January 1863, and his death certificate gives his age as eighty-nine.

Exhibited at the Academy in 1799 (no.5). A portrait of Allnutt's first wife by Lawrence had been exhibited in the previous year.

The pose of the sitter and horse is patently inspired by Reynolds's *Captain Orme* (National Gallery), though in reverse.

Farington (*Diary*, 6 May 1799) records the opinion of Richard Smirke that Shee's portrait of Major Vickars was better than the present picture. Of Lawrence's pictures in the exhibition, his portrait of Miss Jennings attracted most attention. But the portrait of Allnutt was praised in the *St James's Chronicle* (30 April-2 May): '. . . The head is finely painted . . . and the horse extremely well studied'. In the *True Briton* (29 April), copied by *Lloyd's Evening Post* (8-10 May), Lawrence was commended for avoiding his characteristic 'wanton glitter' and for the portrait's 'plain, sober, manly style of colouring, which we advise him to cultivate'.

*Tom Egerton, Esq*

13   *John Allnutt*

14

15

## 14 Margaret, Lady Dundas (1715–1802)

Canvas, 124.5 × 101.7 (49 × 40)
*Provenance*: By family descent.
*Literature*: Garlick, 1954, p.35; 1964, p.71.

The sitter was the daughter of Brigadier-General Alexander Bruce. She married in 1738 Sir Lawrence Dundas, 1st Baronet, a considerable patron of the arts, who died in 1781.

The portrait can be dated well enough to *c*.1799 by a mezzotint of it by George Clint which gives the sitter's age as eighty-four.

*The Marquess of Zetland*

## 15 John Philpot Curran (1750–1817)

Canvas, 73.6 × 60.9 (29 × 24)
*Provenance*: Possibly given by the painter to the 2nd Earl Grey.
*Literature*: Garlick, 1954, p.34; 1964, p.63.

The sitter was an Irish lawyer, MP and a famous orator.

Lawrence painted at least two portraits of Curran, probably towards the end of 1799 or early in 1800. The first of these is now in the National Gallery of Ireland and is usually assumed to be the portrait exhibited at the Academy in 1800 (no.54). According to Williams (I, p.202), Lawrence's first portrait of Curran was a 'failure' and after it was finished he was dining with Curran who became animated, whereupon Lawrence asked to make a second attempt, executed at one sitting. The present picture would appear to be this. If so, it seems to have good claim to be the picture exhibited in 1800, which was publicly praised as a 'spirited performance', with 'fire in the eye', and mentioned as 'finished from one sitting only' (Williams, I, p.203). It is anyway this painting which was engraved by J. R. Smith, not the Dublin one, as rightly recorded by Garlick, 1954, but listed wrongly by him, 1964. The engraving was issued in 1801. A replica or copy was in the sale at Lambton Castle, 18 April 1932 (lot 87).

On 21 December 1799 Farington (*Diary*) called on Lawrence and saw 'an excellent portrait of Curran'.

*Private collection*

16

## 16 George Griffin Stonestreet (1744/5-1802)

Canvas, 127 × 101.7 (50 × 40)
*Provenance*: As commissioned.
*Literature*: Garlick, 1954, p.59; 1964, p.181.

The sitter, born Griffin, adopted his mother's maiden name of Stonestreet in 1794. He was a director of the Phoenix Fire Office and Pelican Life Insurance Office; he wrote a polemical pamphlet, *The Portentous Globe*, 1800. His death in August 1802 is noted in the *Gentleman's Magazine* as occurring in his fifty-seventh year.

A minute of the Phoenix Directors' Board, of 18 December 1799 (kindly communicated by the Company Archivist), expresses gratitude to Stonestreet for various services and records the wish that he sit for his portrait 'to be placed in a conspicuous part of the Premises . . .' The picture was exhibited at the Academy in 1802 (no.421), and is indicated in the catalogue as painted for the Phoenix Assurance Company. Little or no attention was paid to it in newspaper reviews, which singled out among Lawrence's work his *Princess of Wales and Princess Charlotte* (Royal Collection) and *Lady Templetown and her son* (no.17).

A replica of the portrait is noted in the Company archives as having descended in the family of the sitter's daughter.

*Phoenix Assurance Company Ltd*

## 17 Lady Templetown and her son Henry

Canvas, 213.5 × 148.9 (84¾ × 58⅝)
*Provenance*: From the collections of Alfred de Rothschild (d.1918) and the Countess of Carnarvon; acquired by Andrew Mellon.
*Literature*: Garlick, 1954, p.60; 1964, p.185.

Mary, daughter of the 5th Earl of Sandwich, born 1774, married in 1796 the Hon J. H. Upton (succeeded as 2nd Baron Templetown, 1785; created Viscount, 1806); she died in 1824. Her son Henry (1799-1863) succeeded as the 2nd Viscount in 1846.

Exhibited at the Academy in 1802 (no.5); Farington (*Diary*, 21 March 1802) saw it at Lawrence's as one of his exhibits prepared for that year. In the previous year Lawrence had exhibited portraits of Lady Templetown's sisters-in-law, the Hon Sophia and the Hon Caroline Upton, with one of whom, according to Williams (II, p.101), he was much in love at this period.

Some echo of an old master religious composition may lie behind the design; eg a treatment of the *Education of the Virgin* theme. The effect is not unlike that of a contented Hagar with her son in the wilderness.

The *True Briton* (3 May) named the present picture, along with Lawrence's portraits of Lady Conyngham and the Marchioness of Exeter, as 'beautiful proofs of his taste in representing the female character'. On 2 June it added: 'There is more beauty in this picture . . . than in any other of his Works in the present exhibition'. The *Morning Chronicle* (3 May) described it as 'a most beautiful picture'. The *Monthly Mirror* for May declared: 'A highly successful picture of a beautiful woman. It possesses very eminent beauties of softness, clear and simple colour, natural grace, and bright effect.'

The picture was on loan to Lawrence at the time of his death (Executors' List: Garlick, 1964, Appendix IV, no.319).

*National Gallery of Art, Washington*
*(Andrew W. Mellon Collection, 1937)*

17   *Lady Templetown and her son Henry*

## 18 Edmund and Gibbs Antrobus

Canvas, 243.8 × 152.4 (96 × 60)
*Provenance*: By family descent.
*Literature*: Garlick, 1954, p.25; 1964, p.22.

The sitters were the sons of John Antrobus, 2nd son of Philip Antrobus of Congleton, Cheshire. Edmund William (1792-1870) succeeded his uncle as 2nd Baronet in 1826; Gibbs Crawford (1793-1861).

Lawrence exhibited a portrait of 'Mr Antrobus' (probably Edmund, uncle of the sitters here, created 1st Baronet, 1815) at the Academy in 1801 (no.207). The present picture may have been begun about the same time. It was completed by 1802 when a mezzotint of it by George Clint was published.

A later portrait of the younger Edmund Antrobus alone is in the Provost's Lodge, Eton College.

*Sir Philip Antrobus, Bt*

## 19  Lord Thurlow (1732–1806)

Canvas, 125.8 × 100.4 (49½ × 39½)
*Provenance*: Acquired by the Prince Regent.
*Literature*: Garlick, 1954, p.60; 1964, p.186; Millar, no.914.

The sitter, Edward Thurlow, a lawyer of strongly conservative political opinions, rose to become Attorney-General, 1771, and Lord Chancellor (1st Baron Thurlow), 1778. In 1797 he attempted to mediate between the Princess of Wales and the Prince (later Regent), whose adviser he was. He was notorious for his rough manner, to men, and for his consciously old-fashioned dress.

Exhibited at the Academy in 1803 (no.21).Farington records on 12 November 1802 (*Diary*) seeing at Lawrence's 'a very good half-length' of the sitter. On 19 February 1803 he records that Thurlow had 'lately' been sitting to Lawrence, and on 29 March that Lawrence had found the old man 'disposed to converse'. On 7 April Farington sat for a hand in the portrait, 'to complete the ½ length . . . the drapery of which He has begun and finished this day'.

The portrait had first been intended for the Princess of Wales but later in 1803 the Prince obtained it (Farington, *Diary*, 5 October 1803). In June 1814 Lawrence wrote to Colonel McMahon at Carlton House that 'The greatest honor I have ever receiv'd, after the gracious notice of His Majesty, is the having my picture of Lord Thurlow placed in His Royal Highness's collection; and *so* placed as to fill me with the liveliest gratitude . . .' (*Letters of George IV*, ed. A. Aspinall, 1938, I, no.451).

From the first, the picture was greatly admired: by George III, Opie, Fuseli and others. It was, in effect, the portrait of the year at the Academy and recognized as one of Lawrence's best portraits. 'A very fine likeness . . . painted with great solidity of touch and truth of colouring', said the *Star* (2 May). The *Morning Chronicle* (2 May) thought it 'a grand portrait'. The *Daily Advertiser and Oracle* (3 May) said, 'it cannot be praised too much . . . It is a true effigy . . .' The *Morning Post* (30 April) called it the painter's 'best production'. The *British Press or Morning Literary Advertiser* (3 May) said: 'it is, perhaps, a question whether a better portrait in every essential requisite, has ever been produced by the masters of any school on this or that side of the Alps'. One or two newspapers thought the likeness 'a little smoothed and flattered' (*St James's Chronicle*, 3 May); but even these faint demurs were accompanied by much praise.

An unfinished portrait of the sitter was in the Lawrence sale, 18 June 1831 (lot 59).

Williams (I, p.226) believed this was the last portrait

19

painted of Thurlow, but there are two portraits of him by Thomas Phillips (National Portrait Gallery) of 1806.

*Her Majesty The Queen*

## 20  Lord Granville Leveson-Gower, later 1st Earl Granville (1773–1846)

Canvas, 238.8 × 144.8 (94 × 57)
*Provenance*: By family descent.
*Literature*: Garlick, 1954, p.46; 1964, p.125.

The sitter, a diplomat and ambassador, much admired for his good looks, was created Viscount Granville in 1815 and Earl Granville in 1833. He was the youngest son of the 1st Marquess of Stafford and father of the Victorian statesman, the 2nd Earl Granville. At the lower left the arms of Granville, without coronet or supporters, but with the crest (a wolf passant) and the motto: 'Francas non flectes'.

The portrait is dated by Garlick to *c.*1795–1800 but must in fact be altogether rather later. There is a reference to it in a letter of 8 November 1804 from Lady Bessborough to Leveson-Gower, earlier in the year sent as ambassador extraordinary to St Petersburg,

20

## 21 Lady Elizabeth Foster, later Duchess of Devonshire (1759-1824)
*Colour plate III, page 37*

Canvas, 235 × 145 ($92\frac{1}{2}$ × $57\frac{1}{16}$)
*Provenance*: From the collection of Sir Vere Foster;
A. M. Grenfell sale, 26 June 1914 (lot 48), bought by
Sir Hugh Lane, by whom bequeathed to the National
Gallery of Ireland, 1918.
*Literature*: Garlick, 1954, p.37; 1964, pp.67-8.

The sitter, a daughter of the 4th Earl of Bristol, married
first J. T. Foster (d.1795). She was very friendly with
the 5th Duke of Devonshire and also with his Duchess
(d.1806); she married the Duke in 1809. Her last years
were spent in Rome (see below).

Exhibited at the Academy in 1805 (no.195) but little
commented on at the time. Farington (*Diary*) noted
seeing it at Lawrence's on 31 March that year, having
called at the artist's request to look at it. Williams (I,
pp.260-1) seems the first to state that the sitter is shown
as a Sibyl and to identify the view of the temple at
Tivoli in the background – which Lawrence was not to
see until 1819, when he thought the only person who
could do justice to 'such a union of the highly and
varied picturesque . . .' was Turner (Williams, II,
p.160). Traditionally, in post-classical art, the
Tiburtine Sibyl is usually shown revealing the birth of
Christ to the Emperor Augustus, but Lawrence gives
the sitter no more than a pensive, faintly prophetic air.

As Elizabeth, Duchess of Devonshire, she was drawn
in Rome in 1819 by Lawrence, whom she warmly
welcomed there; after her death he wrote (Layard,
p.185, dated to 1826, by a slip): 'I *have* lost a very true
and sincerely valued Friend . . .' It was for her that he
executed the drawing of Cardinal Consalvi (no.83).

which suggests that the portrait had been begun
comparatively recently: 'Lawrence told me (perhaps
by way of flattery) that your Picture had given him
more pleasure than any he ever painted' (*Lord Granville
Leveson-Gower: Private Correspondence, 1781 to 1821*,
ed. Castalia, Lady Granville, 1916, I, p.494). A letter of
Lady Stafford's to Leveson-Gower in the following
year, 1 May 1805, says: 'I have *not* got your Picture.
Lawrence has not touched it since you left England; he
pays no attention to my repeated messages' (op. cit. II,
p.66). There is a reference to the portrait among
Lawrence's own list of pictures painted and painting in
1806 (Garlick, 1964, Appendix II, p.207), and it may be
significant that Farington noted in 1808 (*Diary*, 19
January 1808) that 'yesterday Lord Levison-Gower
. . .was with him' (Lawrence).

When Lawrence was in Paris in 1825 (cf no.44) the
sitter (become Viscount Granville) was ambassador
there and was helpful and friendly.

*Earl Granville*

*National Gallery of Ireland, Dublin*

## 22   Mrs Maguire and her son

Canvas, circular, 165.1 (65) diameter
*Provenance*: By family descent.
*Literature*: Garlick, 1954, p.49; 1964, p.137.

Mrs Maguire was the mistress of the 1st Marquess of Abercorn around 1800; she was known also as Mrs Hawkins. Her son by Lord Abercorn is usually called Arthur Fitzjames but at the time seems to have been called John James Hamilton. From his appearance here he must have been born about 1799.

Exhibited at the Academy in 1806 (no.91) as 'A Fancy group', though the relationship of the sitters to the commissioner was widely known and openly implied in print. It had been painted for Abercorn by the early months of 1805 but he had not wanted the picture exhibited until the following year (Farington, *Diary*, 27 March 1805).

Lawrence had known Abercorn from his earliest days in London: 'an old Jermyn Street friend – a staunch and honourable one', he told his sister in a letter of January 1803 (Williams, I, p.233). A portrait of Abercorn by him had been exhibited at the Academy in 1790 (no.80). Abercorn separated from his second wife in 1798 and remarried in 1800. Farington (*Diary*) noted on 13 December 1803 that Lawrence dined with

him and that a topic of conversation was 'Lord and Lady Abercorn and Mrs Hawkins'.

Farington went to see the picture at Lawrence's and give his opinion on it on 12 February 1805 (*Diary*); he calls the boy John James Hamilton. Abercorn's reluctance to have the portrait exhibited must have been connected with a fear of grave scandal while Mrs Maguire remained in London, but on 2 September 1805 Farington recorded that she was 'to go to Ireland and remove a cause of jealousy'. With her departure Abercorn presumably felt free to let Lawrence exhibit the picture.

Those enthusiastic about it included Fuseli: 'like a charm, having all that *mind* and the *pencil* could do' (Farington, *Diary*, 24 April 1806), and as exhibiting 'exquisite ideas of pleasure without exciting any vicious feelings'. Northcote, however (loc. cit. 6 May 1806), judged that the woman 'looked like a *whore* which was not necessary', and the boy 'as if he had been bred among the vices of an impure house'; he thought Lawrence desired to wear the 'Armour of Rubens . . .'

The *Morning Chronicle* (5 May) found it 'full of colour . . . the heads of the boy and dog are beautiful; but it is deficient in that sobriety and simplicity that give force to a composition . . .' The *St James's Chronicle* (15-17 May) pronounced it 'admirably rich

and highly animated'. The *Sun* (17 May) was among those newspapers which referred to the reluctance of a 'certain nobleman' for the picture to be exhibited in the previous year. 'There is', it continued, 'a playfulness in the arrangement of the group which might rather be expected from brother and sister than from mother and son.' The *Morning Advertiser* (5 May) spoke of the 'beautiful "female friend" of [a noble Marquess]', and said the picture 'possesses all the meretricious beauties' associated with the painter. More than one newspaper criticized the stone-coloured spandrels in which Lawrence had framed it.

From a list containing what seems a reference to this picture ('Mrs Hawkins and child') Lawrence appears to have charged only £50 for it (cf Garlick, 1964, Appendix II, p.270). A drawing of the picture was claimed by Wilkie on behalf of Mr Geddes at Lawrence's death: Executors' List, no.244 (Garlick, 1964, Appendix IV, no.297).

*The Duke of Abercorn*

## 23 Sir Francis Baring, Bt, John Baring and Charles Wall

Canvas, 154.9 × 226.1 (61 × 89)
*Provenance*: By family descent.
*Literature*: Garlick, 1954, p.60; 1964, p.26.

Sir Francis Baring (1740-1810), merchant and founder of the financial house of Baring Brothers; made a baronet, 1793. John Baring (1730-1816) was his brother and Charles Wall his son-in-law (1756-1815). Sir Francis holds a paper inscribed 'Hope & Co', and the name is written on the open page of the ledger held by Wall; it refers to the banking firm of Amsterdam.

Exhibited at the Academy in 1807 (no.210). It was commissioned by Sir Francis Baring and planned as a companion piece to Reynolds's group portrait of Lord Lansdowne, Lord Ashburton and Colonel Barré, which Baring owned. On 13 September 1806 Farington (*Diary*) noted that Lawrence was to go on 30th of the month to Baring's country house, Stratton Hall, to 'paint three Portraits in one picture'. He recorded that Baring spoke of then having three group pictures: of his political friends by Reynolds, of his 'domestic connexions' by West, and Lawrence's painting. Lawrence returned to London, as noted by

COLOUR PLATE IV    *George Hamilton Gordon, 4th Earl of Aberdeen* (no.24)

Farington, on 3 November.

Baring had been deaf from childhood, and that he should be shown as such was commented on somewhat adversely by some newspapers. But both he and Lawrence can hardly have failed to be aware of Reynolds's self-portrait of the 1770s (Tate Gallery), indicating very similarly the same affliction; and Reynolds must have been much in the minds of patron and painter.

The picture seems to be the first commission from Baring to Lawrence but it was followed by several others, for pictures and drawings (cf nos.72 and 73). In turn, Lawrence consulted Baring about this period over his debts and acute financial difficulties (cf Layard, pp.52-5).

Newspaper reviews were largely favourable. The *Star* (7 May) thought it 'one of the best executed conversation pieces the English School has to boast of: in it Mr Lawrence has combined the rich stiles of Van Dyck and Sir Joshua Reynolds'. The *Daily Advertiser* (28 May) said it might be called 'a fine Venetian picture, possessing all the luxuriance and splendour of Paul Veronese'. The *Sun* (5 May) found it 'a remarkably splendid and expressive production', and the *Morning Post* (21 May) said it was 'One of the most splendid compositions of Portraits that has for some time graced the walls of the Academy'. But Lawrence was annoyed by the *Morning Chronicle*, whose editor was James Perry, notoriously a friend of Hoppner's. On 4 May the *Morning Chronicle* called the present picture 'a chef d'oeuvre', while stating that Hoppner fully maintained his title 'to the highest place as a portrait painter'. The following day it declared that Hoppner's portrait of the Prince of Wales, 'like Mr Lawrence's picture of Sir Francis Baring and Family ... is too glaring and shewy'. On the same day Lawrence wrote about this criticism to Farington (Layard, p.45), angrily and somewhat unfairly, that 'of course Mr Perry makes me second to H——r'.

*Private collection, by arrangement with*
*Baring Brothers & Company Ltd*

## 24   George Hamilton Gordon, 4th Earl of Aberdeen (1784-1860)
*Colour plate IV, page 48*

Canvas, 77.4 × 60.9 (30½ × 24)
*Provenance*: By family descent until the transfer of Haddo House to the National Trust for Scotland.
*Literature*: Garlick, 1954, p.23; 1964, p.14.

The sitter travelled in Greece as a young man and then entered politics. He served as Foreign Secretary under Wellington and held various high offices under Peel; he became Prime Minister in 1852 and resigned in 1855. He married as his first wife the daughter of Lawrence's friend, the 1st Marquess of Abercorn (cf no.22), and acted as a pall-bearer at Lawrence's funeral.

Exhibited at the Academy in 1808 (no.74). Lawrence showed it to Farington (*Diary*, 1 April 1808) before the exhibition opened, among pictures he intended to send in. The picturesque 'Byronic' air of the portrait seems not unsuitable for someone apostrophized the following year by Byron as 'The travell'd thane, Athenian Aberdeen' (*English Bards and Scotch Reviewers*). Another, more official portrait of the sitter, commissioned by Peel in 1829, was among the last pictures Lawrence painted (see no.52).

Newspaper attention probably fastened more on Lawrence's posthumous portrait of Pitt at the 1808 exhibition, but the *Examiner* (15 May) found 'great breadth, simplicity and dignity' in the present picture, and the *Morning Chronicle* (2 May) called it 'a good head'.

*The National Trust for Scotland*

Colour Plate V   *Mrs George Stratton* (no.25)

COLOUR PLATE VI   *Lieutenant-General Sir Charles Stewart, later 3rd Marquess of Londonderry* (no.28)

full of praise. The *Morning Chronicle* (29 April) spoke of 'the elegant gracefulness of beauty' in the portrait, but *Bell's Weekly Messenger* (2 June), after mentioning the 'extreme beauty of the lady . . . and the splendour and richness' (of the picture), pronounced it 'somewhat too luxurious . . . It abounds too much in these licentious tones, which are not found within the grave and sober appearances of truth and nature'.

Garlick, 1964, records a small-scale repetition. A large-scale variant, similar in size to the present picture, also exists, recorded in the Seach Collection, Bethel Park, Pennsylvania. A drawing of Mrs Stratton on canvas of about the same date is exhibited here (no.75).

*John and Mable Ringling Museum of Art,*
*Sarasota, Florida*

## 25    Mrs George Stratton (c.1778–1861)
*Colour plate V, page 50*

Canvas, 240.7 × 149.3 (94¾ × 58¾)
*Provenance*: Recorded in the will of Mrs Stratton (1855) as only lent to her and belonging at her death to her nephew the Rev Granville John Granville; sold by the Granville family to Duveen and bought from him, 1927.
*Literature*: Garlick, 1954, p.59; 1964, p.182.

The sitter was Anne, daughter of Bernard d'Ewes, who married George Frederick Stratton of Tew Park, Oxfordshire, in 1805; he was the eldest son of a governor of Madras. Her mother (Ann, née De la Bere) had been a beauty, and in her own circle she was reputed as even more beautiful. She died a widow at Great Malvern, 20 January 1861; her death certificate gives her age as eighty-three.

Exhibited at the Academy in 1811 (no.69). Farington had called on Lawrence on 27 December 1810 (*Diary*) when he saw this portrait; it and another promised to be the best, he thought, of Lawrence's pictures. When he saw it again on 24 January the following year, he noted 'in some respects I thought His best picture'.

Newfoundland dogs were fashionable at the period. When working in the summer of 1811 on the portrait of the Pattisson boys and their donkey (no.32), Lawrence told their mother of the most troublesome sitter he had ever had: 'I once had to paint a Newfoundland dog' (cf M. Hardie in *Magazine of Art*, II, 1904, pp.265 ff) and it seems likely that he was referring to the notably lively dog here.

*Akermann's Repository of Arts* (1 June) thought this picture 'the only conspicuous whole length in the exhibition . . . No one who has seen the original will wonder at so rare an assemblage of excellencies . . .' Some other newspapers and periodicals were equally

## 26    The 6th Duke of Devonshire (1790–1858)

Canvas, 144.8 × 119.4 (57 × 47)
*Provenance*: By family descent.
*Literature*: Garlick, 1954, p.34; 1964, p.68.

William George Spencer Cavendish succeeded his father as 6th Duke in 1811. He was to employ Wyatville and Paxton at Chatsworth, a corner of which is seen at the right of the composition; his patronage of sculptors was also notable (cf J. Kenworthy-Browne in *Apollo*, October 1972, pp.322 ff).

The first intimation of the Duke sitting to Lawrence is a mention by Farington (*Diary*) that 'today', 16 August 1811, 'the young Duke' sat for a half-length portrait. On 19 September he noted that Lawrence spoke favourably of the Duke, 'who has been sitting to him', and mentioned several instances of his 'prudence and good disposition'. These included his generous attitude to the widow of his father's second marriage (see no.21, *Lady Elizabeth Foster*), although he had not approved of the marriage.

In October 1811 Lady Bessborough reported seeing what must have been this portrait in Lawrence's studio: '. . . very like and a fine picture, but the nose rather too thin and the eyes rather too languishing, which is, I think, a fault of Lawrence . . .' (*Lord Granville Leveson-Gower: Private Correspondence, 1781 to 1821*, ed. Castalia, Lady Granville, 1916, II, p.405).

Lawrence exhibited another portrait of the 6th Duke at the Academy in 1824 (no.146). A third portrait, executed for George IV and finished in 1828, is in the Royal Collection (Millar, no.895).

*Private collection*

26    *The 6th Duke of Devonshire*

COLOUR PLATE VII    *William and Jacob Pattisson* (no.32)

COLOUR PLATE VIII    *The Prince Regent, later George IV* (no.33)

27   *Mrs Joseph May*

## 27 Mrs Joseph May (1745-1824)

Canvas, 94 × 73.6 (37 × 29)
*Provenance*: For long in family possession; with
Agnew's, 1971; Mrs T. A. Duncan sale, Christie's
6 April 1973 (lot 109), bought Rogers.
*Literature*: Garlick, 1954, p.50; 1964, p.141; *Burlington
Magazine*, CXIII, December 1971, Suppl, plate xlix.

The sitter was Mary, née Coppendale; she married
Joseph May of Hale House, Hants, and was a widow at
her death (*Gentleman's Magazine*, July-December,
1824, p.285). Her son, Joseph May, junior, married
Frances Maria Stert, who was painted by Lawrence
about the same period as the present picture.

Exhibited at the Academy in 1812 (no.88) and
previously listed by Farington (*Diary*, 7 April 1812)
among the 'capital set of pictures, of superior art . . .'
which he had seen at Lawrence's as destined for the
exhibition. A reference in the *Burlington Magazine*, loc.
cit., to the picture being inscribed on the reverse as
painted in the spring of 1811 has not been checked at
the time of writing and may be a slip for the subsequent
year.

Although Lawrence's work was generally well
received in 1812 (eg '. . . eight very fine portraits', the
*Globe*, 2 May), this portrait does not seem to have been
singled out for special mention.

*Private collection*

## 28 Lieutenant-General Sir Charles Stewart, later 3rd Marquess of Londonderry (1778-1854)

*Colour plate VI, page 51*

Canvas, 127 × 101.7 (50 × 40)
*Provenance*: At one time belonging to Prince
Troubetskoi; afterwards by family descent.
*Literature*: Garlick, 1954, p.59; 1964, p.131; R.A.,
*Bicentenary Exhibition*, London, 1968-9 (no.74).

The sitter, Charles William Stewart, was the half-
brother of Castlereagh and succeeded him as 3rd
Marquess in 1822. He had a dashing career in the
Army, serving for a period as Wellington's adjutant-
general, 1809-12. He was appointed ambassador in
1814 at the Congress of Vienna. He became a good
friend of Lawrence's ('one of the most zealous friends
that ever man had . . .', Lawrence wrote in 1827), and
had him paint several portraits of his family (see no.48).

The sitter wears Hussar uniform and the Peninsular
medal (awarded to him for Talavera, 1809).

The present picture is possibly the portrait, or a
replica of it, exhibited by Lawrence at the Academy in
1813 (no.159). No.165 in the same exhibition was a
portrait by James Ward of Stewart's charger. Lawrence
had exhibited a half-length portrait of Stewart at the
Academy in 1811 (no.88), a portrait about which the
sitter was enquiring as early as 20 June 1810 (R.A.,
MSS Law/1/247) and which seems untraced.

On 13 February 1813 Farington (*Diary*) saw a
second portrait of Stewart at Lawrence's painted for
'Marquis Camden'. Farington thought highly of the
picture, '& recommended him to exhibit it'. The
portrait exhibited was mentioned favourably in several
newspaper reviews; the *Examiner* (13 June), for
example, praising its expression of 'military spirit'. A
reference made by Miss Croft (Layard, pp.254-5) to
Stewart's first wife seeing at Lawrence's the portrait of
him 'in the large fur cap' may refer to the present
composition; Lady Stewart died in 1812.

The design of the second portrait is established by a
stipple engraving of 1813 by J. Hopwood (*Military
Panorama*) and by Meyer's mezzotint of 1814 which
Lawrence sent to the Regent (Farington, *Diary*, 11
May 1814); in the latter, however, the sitter wears the
ribbon and star of the Bath which he was awarded only
in 1813.

The version of the portrait in Marquess Camden's
collection is inscribed along the edge of the sitter's
cloak: *Thos. Lawrence pinx. 1812*.

Lawrence painted Stewart again at Vienna in 1819, a
portrait executed for himself (now also in the
collection of the Marquess of Londonderry).

*The Marquess of Londonderry*

COLOUR PLATE IX    *The Archduke Charles of Austria* (no.37)

COLOUR PLATE X   *Pope Pius VII* (no.38)

### 29  Mrs Wolff (1771?-1829)
*Cover*

Canvas, 128.2 × 102.4 ($50\frac{5}{16}$ × $40\frac{5}{16}$)
*Provenance*: Probably the item in the Pall Mall
Gallery sale, Christie's 20 March 1838 (lot 210); its
later history seems unclear until its possession by
W. W. Kimball.
*Literature*: Garlick, 1954, p.63; 1964, p.202; R.A.,
*Bicentenary Exhibition*, London, 1968-9 (no.181).

The sitter, Isabella Anne, second daughter of Norton
Hutchinson of Woodhall Park, Hertfordshire, married
in 1792 Jens Wolff, Danish Consul in London; she
separated from him in or *c*.1810. Lawrence was
friendly at first with both husband and wife; in the
later years of his and Mrs Wolff's lives his friendship
with her greatly deepened. He told Miss Croft (Layard,
p.244) that while always thinking her very beautiful
and very clever he had only gradually 'entered into the
merit of her character'.

Mrs Wolff's pose is, as often stated, based on that of
the Erythraean Sibyl in Michelangelo's fresco on the
ceiling of the Sistine Chapel; Lawrence owned a study
for this figure (British Museum). Additionally, for Mrs

Wolff's pose, especially her head tilted and resting on
her hand, Lawrence may well have had in mind
Veronese's *S. Helena* (National Gallery), itself based on
an engraving, which appeared in several sales and
which in 1804 made a strong impression on Coleridge,
seeing it at the dealer Commyns in Pall Mall. The more
prominent page of the book studied by Mrs Wolff
shows the Delphic Sibyl from Michelangelo's Sistine
ceiling frescoes; the other page, not previously noted,
shows a male(?) nude, not identifiable as from the same
series, and apparently not by Michelangelo. The book
does not look like an invention by Lawrence, but has
not so far been identified. In the background (extreme
right) is a cast of the statue of *Niobe and her daughter*. Jens
Wolff had collected casts of antique sculpture at his
house, Sherwood Lodge, Battersea; these were for sale
in 1813, and a cast of the *Niobe* was among them (cf
W. T. Whitley, *Art in England 1800-1820*, 1928, p.212).
Mrs Wolff's setting must be approximately that of
Sherwood Lodge, which is explicable by the fact that,
though the picture was not finished until after her
separation from Wolff, it had been begun many years
before.

Exhibited at the Academy in 1815 (no.28).
According to Miss Croft (Layard, pp.243 and 246), the
portrait was started *c*.1803 and 'not gone on with for
twelve years'. It was apparently commissioned by Mrs
Wolff's sister, Mrs Hill, who by 1814 had become
offended by the delay in its completion. Miss Croft and
one of her cousins eventually sat for the 'satin drapery'.

Lawrence also executed a smaller painted portrait of
Mrs Wolff and several drawings of her, the majority in
profile. In his posthumous sale, 19 June 1830 (lot 414)
was a chalk drawing on canvas, *Study of a Lady with a
large Book*, probably related to the present
composition.

In the *Champion* (7 May) the reviewer (Hazlitt) gave
the picture some ambiguous praise; 'a chef d'oeuvre of
[Lawrence's] style . . . enough to make the Ladies vow
that they will never again look at themselves in their
glasses, but only in his Canvasses'. In the *Sun* (19 May)
the picture was unequivocally praised: 'remarkable for
all that delicacy and feeling . . .' The *News* (7 May)
thought it 'almost a miracle in feeling and colour; the
attitude exquisite, and the effect chaste and silvery'.
The picture was also admired at the exhibition by the
Prince Regent (Farington, *Diary*, 14 July 1815).

*The Art Institute of Chicago*
*(Mr and Mrs W.W. Kimball Collection, 1922. 4461)*

## 30   The 1st Duke of Wellington (1769–1852)

Canvas, 91.5 × 71.1 (36 × 28)
*Provenance*: Bequeathed by the Marchioness
Wellesley to the 2nd Duke of Wellington, 1853;
included in the gift to the nation of Apsley House
and its contents by the 7th Duke, 1947.
*Literature*: Garlick, 1954, p.62; 1964, p.193.

Arthur Wellesley, fourth son of the 1st Earl of
Mornington; a lieutenant of foot, 1787; commander
and administrator in India, 1796–1805; victorious in
the Peninsular War, 1808–13; defeated Napoleon at the
Battle of Waterloo, 18 June 1815. He was created Duke
of Wellington, 1814. He later entered politics and was
Prime Minister, 1828–30.

The sitter is shown in Field-Marshal's uniform,
wearing the Garter ribbon, the Golden Fleece and the
Grand Cross of the Bath.

Wellington seems to have sat first to Lawrence
*c*.1814. The first portrait of him Lawrence exhibited
was the full-length, shown at the Academy 1815
(no.109), in the Royal Collection (Millar, no.917),
where Wellington wears all or most of the orders and
decorations he had received up to 1814, including the
Golden Fleece (1812) and the Garter (1813). He was not
made GCB until January 1815.

The present portrait cannot presumably be earlier
than that date and can hardly, in fact, have been painted
before the battle of Waterloo, if Wellington gave
Lawrence a fresh sitting for it – as the quality and
character of the picture would suggest. Wellington left
England for Vienna early in the year, and proceeded
thence to Brussels. His appearance, however, is very
close to that in the full-length for which he had posed
in 1814, and a date of *c*.1815–16 seems likely for the
present picture.

Lawrence painted several other portraits of
Wellington, as well as drawing the Duchess (no.76).
Among the items in his studio at his death was not only
the sword Wellington had carried at Waterloo but also
'A Spanish portrait of the Duke of Wellington'
(Garlick, 1964, Appendix IV, no.354), which it is
tempting to think may have been by Goya.

A copy of the present portrait, said to be by
Rembrandt Peale, is noted by Garlick (1964) as in the
Museum of Fine Arts, Boston.

*Wellington Museum, Apsley House*

COLOUR PLATE XI    *Charles William Lambton* (no.42)

Colour Plate XII   *Lady Robert Manners* (no.46)

31   *The Hon Shute Barrington, Bishop of Durham*

## 31 The Hon Shute Barrington, Bishop of Durham (1734-1826)

Canvas, 152.4 × 121.9 (60 × 48)
*Provenance*: Presumably among the pictures bequeathed by the sitter to the Bishop's Palace, Bishop Auckland.
*Literature*: Garlick, 1954, p.26; 1964, p.28.

The sitter, youngest son of John Shute, 1st Viscount Barrington, was successively Bishop of Llandaff, 1769, Salisbury, 1782 and Durham, 1791 (until his death). The book at his left inscribed: *BIBLIOR/COMP.P.L.* This may be intended for a volume of the polyglot Complutensian Bible bequeathed by him to the British Museum.

Exhibited at the Academy in 1816 (no.47). The Bishop first sat to Lawrence for a portrait exhibited at the Academy in 1796 (no.147), but the family had been aware of Lawrence from an early age. The Bishop's brother, Daines Barrington, who wrote about youthful prodigies, mentioned 'a master Lawrence' in 1781, and on some occasion when the Bishop was sitting to Lawrence, possibly for the present portrait, he told him he owned 'a picture of a dog' done at Devizes when the painter was only eight years old (Williams, I, p.66). At Lawrence's request, he cheerfully gave him 'this juvenile effort'.

At the exhibition of 1816 Lawrence also showed a portrait of the Bishop of London which was praised in the *Sun* (2 May), while it added of the present picture, 'Another good Bishop'. The *Morning Chronicle* (1 May) mentioned 'the Two Bishops', among other pictures, as 'exquisite specimens' of Lawrence's portraiture.

The sitter seems well characterized by what Farington recorded (*Diary*, 3 June 1818) of the impression he made when sitting two years later to Owen, at the age of almost eighty-five: 'chearful and sufficiently active to mount His Horse and ride every day . . . Owen thinks . . . that he has a good share of personal vanity'.

*By courtesy of the Lord Bishop of Durham
and the Church Commissioners for England*

## 32 William and Jacob Pattisson
*Colour plate VII, page 54*

Canvas, 127 × 101.7 (50 × 40)
*Provenance*: Painted for the Pattisson family; anonymous (W. Cooper) sale, Christie's 26 March 1860 (lot 154); later in the Naylor collection, Leighton Hall, Monmouthshire; with Agnew's, 1917. Bequeathed with Polesden Lacey and its contents to the National Trust by the Hon Mrs Ronald Greville, 1942.
*Literature*: Garlick, 1954, p.53; 1964, p.158; *Pictures from National Trust Houses*, Agnew's, 1965 (no.29); St John Gore, in *Polesden Lacey* (National Trust booklet), 1971 (no.11).

William Henry Ebenezer (1801-32) and Jacob Howell (1803-74) were sons of W. H. Pattisson of Witham, Essex. Both became lawyers. The elder son was drowned abroad.

Exhibited at the Academy in 1817 (no.44) but begun as early as 1811; the circumstances of its commissioning and the first sittings are known in some detail, partly through vivid letters from the boys' mother (published in a full account by M. Hardie, *Magazine of Art*, II, 1904, pp.265 ff). The possibility of such a portrait being commissioned was mentioned by Henry Crabbe Robinson in a letter of 9 May 1811 to Mr and Mrs

Pattisson. On 18 June he went with Mrs Pattisson and the elder boy to see Lawrence; and on 26 June Lawrence agreed to paint the two boys. A few days later (on 2 July) Lawrence told Mrs Pattisson: 'I mean Jacob to be feeding the donkey'; he became particularly fond of Jacob, as the livelier boy of the two, and discussed with him the colour of the clothes they would wear in the painting.

However, it was not finished for 1812, as had been envisaged, and Lawrence was still apologizing for its non-completion in 1813. At the end of 1815 he assured the parents that it would 'certainly be completed in this ensuing year', and asked when the donkey might be sent up to London.

A study for the head of William Pattisson is in the Museum of Art, Baltimore, and a copy by Etty of his head in the present picture is in the City Art Gallery, York.

The picture was with Lawrence at the time of his death (Garlick, 1964, Appendix IV, no.313), having been lent to him in or around 1828 for engraving; John Bromley's engraving of the picture as *Rural Amusements* was published in 1831.

An unusually long account of the picture was given in the *Literary Gazette* (10 May 1817) in reviewing the Academy exhibition: '. . . The unison of richness and sobriety; of freedom, taste and truth to nature, at once, reminds us of SIR JOSHUA REYNOLDS . . . [the picture] is marked by his warm feeling, his picturesque disposition and masses, and that sportive play of pencil . . .' More briefly, the *Morning Herald* (15 May) called it 'a charming production' and thought the boys' faces 'bespeak gentle dispositions and minds of a high order'.

*The National Trust, Polesden Lacey*

### 33   The Prince Regent, later George IV (1762–1830)
*Colour plate VIII, page 55*

Canvas, 295 × 204 ($116\frac{1}{8}$ × $80\frac{5}{16}$)
*Provenance*: Presented by the Regent to the Corporation of Dublin.
*Literature*: Garlick, 1964, p.86.

The sitter, George Augustus Frederick, Prince of Wales, eldest son of George III and Queen Charlotte (see no.3), was appointed Regent in 1811 when his father's illness was judged permanent; he became King in 1820. A great collector and outstanding royal patron of the arts, he is rightly thought of in connection with Lawrence, though he seems not to have directly commissioned work from him before 1814; from then onwards he was Lawrence's greatest patron, and some of Lawrence's finest portraits were executed for him (see nos.35, 37 and 38) as well as of him.

The Regent is shown in Garter robes and wearing the collar and badge of the Order, as well as the collars of the Guelphic Order and the Bath. He is posed beside the *Table des Grands Capitaines*, commissioned by

Napoleon and given to the Regent by Louis XVIII in 1817. The setting may be intended vaguely for Carlton House.

Exhibited at the Academy in 1818 (no.61). It was shown as a centrepiece, flanked by Dawe's portraits of Princess Charlotte and Prince Leopold.

The Regent first sat to Lawrence in 1814, for a full-length in field-marshal's uniform painted for the future 3rd Marquess of Londonderry (cf no.28) and shown at the Academy in 1815 (no.65). The pose in the present picture is very similar, though oddly the Regent's head seems smaller, his figure slimmer and his features younger; he may well have sat again to Lawrence for this second portrait, the prime original, which became the standard composition for all the many official portraits of him until the end of his reign (the imperial crown replacing the Garter hat after 1820). It should however be noted that he must have given Lawrence a fresh sitting for the subsequent autograph versions (eg Vatican Pinacoteca, Rome), in which the face is fatter and more florid than in the present portrait, and the general effect of it nearer, presumably, to the sitter's appearance in his mid-fifties. It is worth comparing his face here with the portrait by Lawrence of him as King (fig.3), of only four years later.

Miss Croft (Layard, p.252) recollected that when the present picture was sent to Dublin, she learnt that the lower part of the figure, 'the left leg in particular', was considered badly painted and unfinished, and that an Irish painter was to be employed to improve it. Lawrence angrily intervened, though 'He could not help laughing at the absurdity of the thing . . .'

In fact, somewhat similar criticisms had been heard in England, according to *Akermann's Repository of Arts* (June 1818), which declared: 'We suspect . . . that what has been deemed a fault is a high perfection', going on to praise 'the astonishing effect . . . The robes are wonderfully painted . . . The painting in every part of the picture is exquisite . . .' The *Literary Chronicle* (11 May) thought it 'dignified and graceful . . . admirably composed, and beautifully painted'. The *London Chronicle* (2-4 May) called it 'very magnificent' and supposed the background to represent Carlton House. The *British Press* (12 May) detected 'a little flattery in [the] portrait' but also warmly praised 'the colouring of the robes, the breadth of drapery, and the exquisite richness and harmony . . .'

*The City of Dublin*

**34 Lady Elizabeth Leveson-Gower, later Marchioness of Westminster (1797-1891)**

Canvas, 72.4 × 59.6 (28½ × 23½)
*Provenance*: By family descent.
*Literature*: Garlick, 1954, p.46; 1964, p.125.

The sitter, second daughter of the 1st Duke of Sutherland, married in 1819 Richard, Viscount Belgrave (later 2nd Marquess of Westminster).

Exhibited at the Academy in 1818 (no.53). Lady Elizabeth Leveson-Gower lived long enough to give some recollections of sitting to Lawrence ('what struck me most . . . was the *perfection* of the *drawing* of his portraits before any colour was put on – the drawing itself was so perfectly beautiful . . .') to her nephew, Lord Ronald Sutherland Gower, who printed them in *Sir Thomas Lawrence*, 1900, p.110.

The portrait was praised by the *Champion* (11 May): 'A charming head, with a sweet unaffected expression, and an elegant simplicity of attitude', but it complained that Lawrence neglected every part of his pictures except the head. The *Literary Chronicle* (11 May) thought it 'one of those enchanting female heads of which Lawrence always gives us some specimen . . .' Other newspapers mentioned the picture more briefly but favourably.

Two repetitions are recorded by Garlick, 1964, loc. cit.

*The Countess of Sutherland*

## 35 Alexander I, Tsar of Russia (1777-1825)

Canvas, 273 × 179.1 (107½ × 70½)
*Provenance*: Painted for the Prince Regent.
*Literature*: Garlick, 1954, p.24; 1964, p.16; Millar, no.883.

The sitter succeeded his father, Tsar Paul I, in 1801. After being the ally of Prussia and Austria, he was won over to Napoleon but broke with him and joined the European powers who defeated him. As one of the Allied sovereigns, he came to England in 1814 and was warmly welcomed. At once enlightened and despotic, an idealist and an autocrat, he was a puzzle to his contemporaries and to some extent remains one.

He is shown in the uniform of a Russian Field-Marshal, wearing the sword of the Order of the Sword of Sweden and the star of St Andrew of Russia on the Garter ribbon; among his badges are those of the Order of St George of Russia, the Iron Cross of Prussia and the Russian campaign medal of 1812.

The portrait was commissioned by the Regent when the Tsar arrived in London in June 1814, along with the King of Prussia. The original proposal, mentioned by Farington (*Diary*, 11 May 1814), had been for a group portrait of the Regent with the Tsar and the King, but separate portraits were finally decided on. The Russian and Prussian military commanders Platov and Blücher also sat to Lawrence during the summer of 1814, at the Regent's wish. These commissions formed the nucleus of what became the Waterloo Chamber series.

Almost certainly the Tsar did not have time to sit to Lawrence in London. He appears to have met him first at Aix-la-Chapelle four years later. An interesting letter of 6 March 1816 from the future 3rd Marquess of Londonderry to Lawrence (Layard, pp.100-1) refers to 'your *still* anxious desire to paint the Autocrat . . . He would be more ready to give you *at your leisure* sittings at St Petersburg'. In fact, Lawrence waited until the congress of sovereigns and statemen assembled at Aix in the autumn of 1818. There the Tsar gave him seven sittings. Lawrence's own letters (Williams, II, pp.109 ff, and Layard, pp.136–41) record the evolution of the portrait, and reactions to it, in considerable detail. He began with a drawing which he later sent to Angerstein (not Farington, as in Millar); the painting was based on this, but eventually Lawrence spent time 'carefully finishing the drawing *from* the picture', claiming he had adhered 'as closely to truth and identity as I have ever done in any portrait that I have ever painted . . .' (Williams, II, p.126).

The Tsar wore the uniform he had worn at the battle of Leipzig (1813), to which the smoky background probably alludes. Lawrence liked the Tsar and studied him very carefully: 'He stands always resting on one leg . . . either with his hat in his hand or with his hands closely knit before him'. The finished portrait was greatly admired by the Tsar's mother, who commissioned a replica (Hermitage, Leningrad).

Lawrence was aware (Farington, *Diary*, 28 October 1815) that the Tsar had already been painted by Gérard in a portrait much approved of, as also by George Dawe, whose first portrait of the Tsar dates from 1817, and he is likely to have relished the implied challenge – especially as he found Dawe 'prowling . . . *creeping*' around at Aix.

The portrait was still in Lawrence's studio at his death.

*Her Majesty The Queen*

35    *Alexander I, Tsar of Russia*

## 36 John Bloomfield, later 2nd Baron Bloomfield (1802–79)

Canvas, 75.6 × 63.8 (29¾ × 25⅛)
*Provenance*: Bequeathed by the sitter's widow, 1905.
*Literature*: Garlick, 1954, p.28; 1964, p.38;
R. Ormond, *Early Victorian Portraits* (*National Portrait Gallery Catalogue*), 1973, I, p.42.

John Arthur Douglas Bloomfield, diplomat, son of Sir Benjamin (later 1st Baron) Bloomfield, Private Secretary for a period to George IV. He joined the Diplomatic Service in 1818 and was attached first to the embassy at Vienna. He succeeded his father in 1846.

Exhibited at the Academy in 1820 (no.88). Lawrence moved on from Aix (cf no.35) to Vienna in December 1818. Garlick dates this portrait to 1818. It is listed by Lawrence in a letter from Rome of 19 May 1819 (Williams, II, p.145) as among work done during his stay at Vienna, and seems at least as likely to have been done in 1819. The pose in profile to the left was utilized by Lawrence at exactly the same period for his portrait of Lord (Sir) Charles Stewart (cf under no.28).

A copy is in a Scottish private collection (Ormond, loc. cit.).

*National Portrait Gallery, London*

## 37 The Archduke Charles of Austria (1771–1847)

*Colour plate IX, page 58*

Canvas, 269.9 × 178.4 (106¼ × 70¼)
*Provenance*: Painted for the Prince Regent.
*Literature*: Garlick, 1954, p.31; 1964, p.53; Millar no.891.

The Archduke Charles, a younger brother of the Emperor Francis I (also painted by Lawrence), was a talented soldier and Commander-in-Chief of the Austrian armies. He is shown wearing the Golden Fleece and the ribbon and star of the Order of Maria Theresa.

The portrait was painted at Vienna in the early months of 1819. Garlick in both citations gives the date as 1818, but Lawrence seems to mention the Archduke first in a letter of 10 January 1819: 'of small figure, and of dignified, pleasing manners with a face of great strength of character . . .' (Williams, II, p.136). An illness of the Archduke's interrupted the sittings after the portrait had been begun, and Lawrence wrote that this 'detain'd me at Vienna till past Holy Week; for I could not think of leaving it with the Picture of so distinguished a Personage unfinished . . . and I had sittings from him, which enabled me greatly to improve the resemblance . . .' (Williams, II, p.175).

Millar points out that the design appears based on Valentine Green's engraving, published in 1781, of Trumbull's portrait of George Washington; although Lawrence disposed his sitter's hands and sword differently, the general derivation is patent.

Lawrence also began at Vienna a portrait of the Archduchess Charles ('a very sweet, amiable and lovely being'); this was not for the Prince Regent but, as Lawrence himself stated, 'for the Emperor'.

The Archduke's portrait was still in Lawrence's studio at his death.

*Her Majesty The Queen*

### 38 Pope Pius VII (1742-1823)
*Colour plate X, page 59*

Canvas, 269.2 × 177.9 (106 × 70)
*Provenance*: Painted for the Prince Regent.
*Literature*: Garlick, 1954, p.54; 1964, p.162; Millar, no.909; R.A., *Bicentenary Exhibition*, London, 1968–9 (no.186); M. Levey, *Burlington Magazine*, CXVII, 1975, pp.194 ff.

Luigi Barnaba Chiaramonti was elected Pope in 1800; he was present at the coronation of Napoleon in 1801 but later excommunicated him, was arrested by the French and taken first to Fontainebleau. Under pressure of events Napoleon released him in 1814. The Allied sovereigns restored the papal territories and also the works of art ceded by the Vatican to the French.

The throne surmounted by the Chiaramonti arms, with the motto 'Pax'. At the left the archway inscribed: . . . *AVIT [P]IUS VII · PONT · MAX*; the *Apollo Belvedere*, *Laocöon* and the *Torso Belvedere* visible through it. The paper held by the Pope inscribed: *Per/Ant° Canova*.

The portrait was painted at Rome in 1819. Lawrence had his first audience with the Pope on 18 May, having previously presented his credentials to the Pope's chief minister, Cardinal Consalvi (see no.83), whom he was also commissioned to paint for the Regent. He found the Pope sympathetic, benevolent and surprisingly lively. Pius VII gave him nine sittings, and the picture was finished by September. Lawrence's letters home (Williams, II, pp.143, ff, and Layard, pp.144-50) describe his progress on the portrait and his sense of its success: 'it is thought the best and happiest resemblance of the Pope that has ever been painted'. He was particularly aware of David's portraits of Pius VII and also that by Camuccini, 'an image of respectable decay'.

The architecture at the left probably refers to the Braccio Nuovo of the Vatican, built under Pius VII but opened only after Lawrence had left Rome. The sculptures shown were not housed in it, but the *Apollo Belvedere* and the *Laocöon* were among those works which, under British pressure, had been returned from Paris to Rome in 1815. Millar suggests that the paper held by the Pope may be the document creating Canova Marchese d'Ischia, but perhaps it is rather that appointing him Prefect of the Fine Arts at Rome.

The picture was exhibited at the Quirinal Palace before Lawrence left the city and was generally much praised. It was still in Lawrence's studio at his death, but had been seen and admired by several of his artist friends and other visitors (for Sir Walter Scott's eloquent tribute to it, see Levey, loc. cit.). The Pope apparently commissioned a copy of it from Lawrence. George IV sent the Pope the portrait of himself in Garter robes now in the Vatican, based on the design of no.33.

A small replica and two copies by John Simpson are recorded by Garlick, 1964.

A mezzotint of the picture by Cousins was published in 1828; it prompted Delacroix's article on Lawrence in the *Revue de Paris*, June 1829.

*Her Majesty The Queen*

39   *Mrs Henry Baring with two of her children*

## 39 Mrs Henry Baring with two of her children

Canvas, 194.3 × 195.5 (76½ × 77)
*Provenance*: From the collection of the Comtesse de
Noailles (granddaughter of Mrs Baring), Christie's
16 December 1911 (lot 108), bought Wertheimer; his
sale, Christie's 18 June 1920 (lot 27); later with Mrs
Ogden Mills, New York.
*Literature*: Garlick, 1954, p.26; 1964, p.27.

Maria Matilda, second daughter of William Bingham
of Philadelphia, married Henry Baring, third son of Sir
Francis Baring, Bt (see no.23), in 1802. Her sister Anne
had previously married Baring's brother Alexander.
The marriage was dissolved before 1825, and Henry
Baring married again. The identity of the two children
is doubtful, but the boy seems more likely to be the
second son, James Drummond (d.1901); the girl might
be either Anna-Maria, the elder daughter, or her sister
Emily.

Exhibited at the Academy in 1821 (no.106), but
begun several years earlier. In the original composition
Henry Baring was included, presumably behind the
sofa (and cf the drawing of the Allnutt family, no.71
here). Lawrence mentioned the picture to Farington
(*Diary*) on 2 February 1817, when it still was of 'Mr and
Mrs Henry Baring', explaining why 'He shd not finish
it for the ensuing Exhibition'. It may indeed have been
difficulties between Mr and Mrs Baring which had
partly delayed it. At some point the figure of Henry
Baring was suppressed and, apparently, cut out (in
Lawrence's studio at his death was 'Port of [Baring] cut
out of a larger picture' (Garlick, 1964, Appendix IV,
no.191), which Baring claimed).

The picture was well received. The *Observer* (10
June) found 'much natural ease in the attitude of the
lady; and the children are also well executed', but
thought the sky 'unnatural'. The *Englishman* (13 May)
called it 'a large fanciful groupe, well designed, and
brilliantly ornamented and coloured'. The *Magazine of
the Fine Arts* said it was 'a splendid display of the
President's talents in grouping a family picture'. The
*Examiner* (20 May) could, amid other praise, recollect
'no picture of a similar subject from any hand that has
given us more satisfaction'.

*Baring Brothers & Company Ltd*

## 40 The 6th Duke of Bedford (1766-1839)

Canvas, 74.9 × 64.2 (29½ × 24½)
*Provenance*: Originally at Woburn, later sold and
reacquired, Christie's 26 May 1906 (lot 101).
*Literature*: Garlick, 1954, p.27; 1964, pp.31-2.

John, 6th Duke of Bedford, succeeded his brother as
Duke in 1802. He took an interest in agriculture,
natural history and art.

Exhibited at the Academy in 1822 (no.113).
Although not discussed by the newspapers at any
length, the portrait was included in general praise of
Lawrence's 'good likenesses' this year and named as an
example of his even exceeding 'his former beauty of
pencilling and look of life'.

A version, as probably studio work, is recorded by
Garlick in the Marquess of Lansdowne's collection.

*The Marquess of Tavistock and the
Trustees of the Bedford Estates*

## 41  Emily and Laura Anne Calmady

Canvas, 78.4 × 76.5 (30⅞ × 30⅛)
*Provenance*: V. P. Calmady (the sitters' brother) sale, Christie's 22 May 1886 (lot 115), bought in; he died, 1896; entered the collection of Collis P. Huntington, New York, by whom bequeathed.
*Literature*: Garlick, 1954, p.30; 1964, pp.46-7.

Emily (1818-1906?) and Laura Anne (1820-94) were the eldest children of Charles Biggs Calmady of Langdon Hall, Devon. Laura Anne is recorded as dying in 1894, aged seventy-four; she made her will in that year, mentioning her sister Emily, but there seems no record of Emily's death, at least in England, and the date here is that usually stated in the literature.

Exhibited at the Academy in 1824 (no.99). The engraver F. C. Lewis first suggested to Mrs Calmady that her two children should be painted, and Lawrence saw them in July 1823. He made a chalk drawing of them, full face (engraved by Lewis) which, according to Williams (II, p.336), he gave to their mother. He probably made some other drawings or sketches, and was sufficiently charmed by the children to have them at meals. Mrs Calmady made a drawing of his studio (fig.1) at the time he was painting the picture. At one point he had one of Laura Calmady's shoes taken off to give greater intimacy and vivacity – and perhaps something of this effect lingers in the painting. Although Lawrence aimed at a totally 'natural' impression, he may have been inspired in the composition, consciously or not, by Italian sixteenth- and seventeenth-century paintings of the Infant Christ with St John the Baptist; even the tondo form seems a recollection of 'old master' pictures, and the ultimate inspiration probably lies in Raphael's *Madonna della Sedia*.

The picture was enthusiastically received in all the main newspapers. The *Examiner* (10 May) could not conceive 'any genius short of a Corregio's [sic] capable of surpassing [it]'. The *London Magazine* (June) thought it 'might vie in expression with any picture of a similar subject of any age', though it mistook the younger girl for a boy. *The Times* (4 May) found it one of Lawrence's 'happiest works . . . and by the playfulness of his pencil [he] has given a degree of motion to their graceful forms'. The *County Literary Chronicle* (8 May) declared it beyond all praise 'for expression and sentiment, execution and colouring'. The *Literary Gazette* (8 May) called it 'a focus of talent . . . Powerful and glittering as it is in execution, the playful and beautiful sentiment that shines through all is its greatest charm'.

The picture was sent to Windsor for the King to see in October 1824, and Lawrence told Mrs Calmady of his interest in it (Williams, II, pp.342-3). It was with Lawrence in Paris in 1825 and was possibly exhibited by him while there (cf *Memoirs and Recollections of the late Abraham Raimbach, Esq*, ed. M. T. S. Raimbach, 1843, p.128).

Three lots in the Lawrence sale on 18 June 1831 (76, 77 and 87) may have been studies for or related to the composition. Garlick, 1964, records a copy in the Musée Cognac-Jay, Paris.

*Metropolitan Museum of Art, New York*
*(Bequest of Collis P. Huntington, 1925)*

**42 Charles William Lambton (1818-31)**
*Colour plate XI, page 62*

Canvas, 137.2 × 111.8 (54 × 44)
*Provenance*: By family descent.
*Literature*: Garlick, 1954, p.45; 1964, p.120; R.A., *Bicentenary Exhibition*, London, 1968-9 (no.182).

The sitter was the eldest son of J. G. Lambton (later 1st Earl of Durham). His parents admired his precocious intelligence as well as his appearance. Miss Croft (Layard, pp.258-9) recorded encountering him at Lawrence's: 'The beautiful young Lambton I once met . . . so as to be able to pronounce the picture not a jot more lovely than he was'. His health began to cause concern as early as 1826.

Exhibited at the Academy in 1825 (no.288). An apparently undated letter from Lady Louisa Lambton, the sitter's mother, to her husband speaks of being 'just returned with Charles from his sitting. Sir Thomas has drawn in the figure very carefully, and is to have a very long sitting the next time . . . I don't see how anything can look better than the dress' (cf S. J. Reid, *Life and Letters of the Earl of Durham*, 1906, I, p.184).

A not unmalicious mention in *News of Literature and Fashion*, 1825 (cf W. T. Whitley, *Art in England, 1821-1837*, 1930, pp.88-9), refers to the sitter having first been painted in yellow. This may have been so, though the colour is not very typical of Lawrence, and might have looked odd combined with the moonlight effect. The high, rocky setting and the river below may hint at the family's association with Durham; it may also have significance for Lawrence, who wrote a poem, *On a drawing of a boy climbing a rock*, with the verse:

> Proceed, dear boy, and climb the hill,
> Enjoy the morning of thy time
> And all the rocks of future life
> As cheerful and as active climb.

The picture was favourably reviewed but possibly less enthusiastically than had been the Calmady children (no.41) of the previous year. The *Monthly Magazine* (June) confessed to not understanding 'a spot of light in a corner ... it looks like a peep of the moon ...' The *Morning Herald* (3 May) thought the air of 'lofty contemplation' not in accord with youth, though the *Parthenon* (11 June) found the portrait 'a very model of youthful intelligence ... the ... subject ... seemed not to be of paint, but to live, to breathe, to think'. *The Times* (3 May) said 'The countenance beams with the sparkling intelligence ...' More than one newspaper spoke of the delight in turning to the picture from Danby's *Delivery of Israel out of Egypt*, which hung below it.

The picture was exhibited at the Paris Salon in 1827. A letter from Thomas Jones to Lawrence (postmarked 7 December 1827) quotes from a French newspaper, '*Le portrait ... attire les regards de la foule*', and records a visitor saying that it was Lawrence's '*idéal*' of Lord Byron when a child (R.A., MSS Law/5/197).

A copy was given by Lambton, *c*.1837, to his father-in-law, the 2nd Earl Grey (cf Reid, op. cit. II, p.123) who found it 'little, if at all, inferior to the original'.

The composition probably influenced various later portraits of boys (and may itself be partly inspired by Archer Shee's portrait of his son, William; Royal Academy) and seems consciously echoed in Millais's *Hon John Neville Manners* (d.1896), anonymous sale, Christie's 25 May 1979 (lot 82).

*Lord Lambton*

43

### 43  Princess Sophia (1777–1848)

Canvas, 141.6 × 113.7 (55¾ × 44¾)
*Provenance*: Painted for George IV.
*Literature*: Garlick, 1954, p.58; 1964, p.179; Millar, no.880.

The sitter was the thirteenth child of George III and Queen Charlotte. She died unmarried. She suffered from poor sight and became blind in her last years.

She wears on her left shoulder a jewelled miniature of George IV. An eyeglass is tucked into her waist-band.

Exhibited at the Academy in 1825 (no.57). A letter from Lawrence to his nephew, possibly of January 1825 (Williams, II, p.404), mentions having just written to the sitter, 'whom the King has commanded me to paint'. Lawrence asked for permission to exhibit the picture at the Academy, and Lord Conyngham replied on 4 April 1825 (R.A., MSS Law/4/314) that though the King 'does not usually approve of portraits

44

## 44  The Duchesse de Berry (1798–1870)

Canvas, 91 × 71 ($35\frac{13}{16}$ × $27\frac{15}{16}$)
*Provenance*: Acquired in France, 1976.

Marie-Caroline (Maria Carolina), eldest daughter of Francis I of the Two Sicilies, married Charles, Duc de Berry, son of Charles X of France, in 1816; he was assassinated in 1820.

The sitter was a leader of fashion and was painted by Gérard and Lefèvre, among other artists. She wears a tartan toque – part of the fondness in France at the period for things Scottish. She suffered from a defect in her vision, as Lawrence tactfully hints, and holds an eyeglass.

Lawrence arrived in Paris in August 1825 to paint Charles X for George IV. At some of the sittings were the children of the Duchesse de Berry, and on 4 September he wrote to (probably) Lord Conyngham seeking the King's permission to paint a threequarter-length of the Duchesse who had personally requested this after seeing some of his portraits (R.A., MSS Law/4/367). On 20 October he wrote to Mrs Wolff (Layard, p.199) to say that the first sitting had not yet taken place but that it had to be delayed 'for a few Days'.

It seems likely that Lawrence painted two versions of the portrait. One, now in a private collection, England, is Garlick, 1954, p.28; 1964, p.35; that picture apparently belonged to the Comte de Forbin, a friend of Ingres and Director-General of the Museums under Charles X. The earlier provenance of the present picture is not established.

A copy is in the Musée Crozatier, Le Puy.

*Musée National du Château de Versailles et Trianon*

being exhibited', he would in this instance oblige Lawrence.

The *Literary Chronicle* (7 May) called it 'a charming picture, the drapery of which is managed with exquisite skill'. The *European Magazine* (May) said, 'a splendid, and, at the same time, delicate work'. *Akermann's Repository of Arts* (1 June) thought little justice was done to the Princess's features and complexion, but 'this is the only imperfect part of the portrait; for the attitude is full of ease and dignity, and the rich and magnificent colouring of the dress, and the beauty of its folds, are naturally and suitably managed'. The *Examiner* (19 June) particularly praised the flesh tints, 'in their pearly delicacy, rivalling the best in modern painting'. The *London Magazine* (June) thought the picture 'not less remarkable for its easy elegance of attitude, than for its correct resemblance to the original, and its splendid display of colour'.

*Her Majesty The Queen*

45    *Sir Henry Halford, Bt*

## 45 Sir Henry Halford, 1st Bt (1766-1844)

Canvas, 142.2 × 111.8 (56 × 44)
*Provenance*: Presented by Sir Henry St John Halford, 3rd Bt, 1897.
*Literature*: Garlick, 1954, p.40; 1964, p.98.

The sitter was born Vaughan and took the name Halford. A highly successful physician, he attended George IV, William IV and Queen Victoria, and also visited Lawrence in his final illness. He was created a baronet in 1809, and was President of the Royal College of Physicians from 1820 until his death. He is shown wearing the star of the Hanoverian Order and with his President's gown hanging on the back of his chair.

There seems no record of when Halford sat to Lawrence, but the picture can hardly date from before 1825, in which year Halford was made Knight Commander of the Hanoverian Order. The occasion of this was the move that year of the College to Pall Mall East on a site of land granted by the Crown, and it may well have been at this date that Halford chose to be painted.

*Royal College of Physicians*

46

## 46 Lady Robert Manners (1737-1829)
*Colour plate XII, page 63*

Canvas, 138.8 × 110.5 ($54\frac{5}{8}$ × $43\frac{1}{2}$)
*Provenance*: By family descent; bequeathed by Mrs Nisbet Hamilton Ogilvy of Biel, 1921.
*Literature*: Garlick, 1954, p.49; 1964, p.138.

Mary, only daughter of Colonel Thomas Digges, married Lord Robert Manners, fifth child of John, 2nd Duke of Rutland, in 1756. The sitter had been painted by Allan Ramsay some seventy years before the present portrait; cf C. Thompson, *Pictures for Scotland: the National Gallery of Scotland and its Collection . . .*, 1972, p.109.

Exhibited at the Academy in 1826 (no.75). Garlick (1954, p.13) has detected the influence of Velazquez's 'portraits of the Infantas' at Vienna in the dominant blue colour of the present picture; in this connection it might possibly be that the vase of flowers, an uncommon adjunct in Lawrence's portraits, is some recollection of the vase of flowers in the portrait of the Infanta Margarita in pink. A fainter and perhaps only accidental affinity seems to exist between the present portrait and Rembrandt's threequarter-length of Margaretha Trip (National Gallery, London), extending to the device of the sitter's handkerchief introduced into the composition. Although the Rembrandt was in England, it was not publicly exhibited until after Lawrence's death. Closer still in affinity is the portrait of Elizabeth Jacobsdr. Bas (Rijksmuseum, Amsterdam), now attributed to Bol but then accepted as a Rembrandt; it belonged to W. F. Mogge Muilman, who had been painted by Lawrence.

Lawrence was recognized by reviewers in 1826 as outstanding for his 'mental portraiture' (*The Times*, 29 April) and for possessing 'The most perfect style' (*Akermann's Repository of Arts*, 1 June) but surprisingly little notice was given to this portrait except for a vague phrase in the *Examiner* (11 June): 'Sentiments of respect are raised by the venerable presence of . . . Lady R. Manners'.

*National Gallery of Scotland, Edinburgh*

## 47 John Nash (1752-1835)

Canvas, 137.2 × 110.5 (54 × 43½)
*Provenance*: Painted for Jesus College, Oxford, at the request of Nash in lieu of payment for work there.
*Literature*: Garlick, 1954, p.52; 1964, p.149.

The sitter, a distinguished architect especially of London, was much patronised by George IV before and after his accession; his work and his character were frequently stigmatized by his contemporaries, and the Duke of Wellington successfully opposed the King's wish to confer on him a baronetcy.

The setting of the portrait seems clearly meant for that of the gallery in the house Nash designed for himself at No.14 Regent Street (cf the plate from Britton and Pugin's *Illustrations of the Public Buildings of London*, 1825-7, reproduced in J. Summerson, *John Nash*, 1935, plate XII). Nash used to work in this gallery, at the entrance to which stood casts of the *Apollo Belvedere* and the Louvre *Artemis*, the latter positioned at the left, as summarily indicated in the background here. Lawrence too owned casts of both statues (cf the plate facing p.90 in Layard).

Exhibited at the Academy in 1827 (no.314). Among Lawrence's exhibits in the same year was *Mrs Peel* (cf fig.4 and no. 89) which inevitably attracted far more attention. The *Morning Post* (29 May) found in the *Nash* 'the likeness . . . perfect' but the background 'which exhibits some architectural interest . . . less satisfactory'. It went on to compare the background introduced here with that 'done with great success' in the portrait of Pius VII (no.38): '. . . the objects to be introduced are very inferior'. The *Examiner* (24 June) said 'Nature has amply compensated this gentleman, by gifting his mind instead of his face, if it is a portrait of the able architect of that name; and the painter has displayed that refinement of mind . . . Sir Thomas always exhibits the mind'.

*The Principal and Fellows of Jesus College, Oxford*

## 48 Frances, Marchioness of Londonderry, (1800–65), and her son, Viscount Seaham

Canvas. c.254 × 152.4 (c. 100 × 60)
*Provenance*: By family descent.
*Literature*: Garlick, 1954, p.48; 1964, pp.131–2.

Frances Anne, daughter of Sir Henry Vane Tempest, Bt, of Wynyard, married Lord Charles Stewart as his second wife in 1819. Their eldest son, George Henry, Viscount Seaham (1821-84) became 5th Marquess of Londonderry in 1872.

A half-length of Lady Londonderry had been commissioned from Lawrence in 1818. Lord Seaham was painted by him as an infant (R.A., 1824 (no.392)).

Exhibited at the Academy in 1828 (no.140) and probably painted, or begun, in the previous year. Lawrence stayed with Londonderry at his Doncaster house during 1827, though the occasion was social ('. . . the company', he wrote, 'is only all London, with the slight addition of all Yorkshire and Derbyshire . . .').

The pose of Lady Londonderry, ascending a step towards the left, with right arm extended, must derive from the Van Dyck design which was engraved and used in, for instance, his *Beatrice de Cusance, Princess of Cantecroix* (Royal Collection). The composition and general air of the picture also suggest some distinct influence on Lawrence of French portraiture of the period, especially the work of Gérard, with whom he had been on very friendly terms in Paris in 1825. Gérard's *Madame Visconti* (Louvre), of 1810, may be compared.

At Lawrence's death a sketch of Lord Seaham was in his studio ('included in the price of the large picture last year': Garlick, 1964, Appendix IV, no.101); Garlick implies that this was the portrait shown at the Academy in 1824, but it seems more likely to have been a sketch directly related to the present picture.

The *Literary Chronicle* (10 May) thought the picture 'would rivet the attention of all', but for the competition of Lawrence's *Countess Gower and her daughter*, which hung near it. The *London Magazine* (June) said that though there might be felt to be 'too much redundancy and lubricity to the character of the painting', the Marchioness was 'represented as exceedingly fair and attractive; the composition is somewhat in the style of Sir Joshua'. The *Examiner* (18 May) mentioned Lord Seaham among examples of 'better character' in Lawrence's portraits of children (to which 'he has sometimes given too much importance and artificialness of air'). The *Athenaeum* (7 May) described the picture as 'elegant' but not the equal of *Countess Gower*: 'the action of the boy is wanting in grace . . .'

*The Marquess of Londonderry*

47   *John Nash*

48   *Frances, Marchioness of Londonderry, and her son, Viscount Seaham*

## 49  William Wilberforce (1759-1833)

Canvas, 96.5 × 109.2 (38 × 43)
*Provenance*: Presented by the executors of Sir Robert Harry Inglis, Bt, 1857.
*Literature*: Garlick, 1954, pp.62-3; 1964, pp.197-8.

The sitter, reformer, philanthropist and MP first for Hull, later for Bramber, became Parliamentary leader in the cause for the abolition of slavery in 1787; the bill for abolition, often rejected, received the royal assent in 1807. He is shown holding an eyeglass.

The portrait was commissioned by Sir Robert Harry Inglis from Lawrence in 1825, the year Wilberforce retired from Parliament. A letter of 8 April 1826 from him to the artist (R.A., MSS Law/5/13) refers to having lately reminded Wilberforce of 'the promise you were so good as to make me last year', that Wilberforce should sit to him, and hopes the summer will not pass without arrangements 'to complete such a work'. (When Lawrence was abroad in 1819 Wilberforce had expressed to Farington (*Diary*, 17 August 1819) 'great pleasure' at Lawrence's reception at foreign courts.)

Wilberforce sat for 'the first time for Inglis; had a very pleasant hour', on 14 May 1828, as he noted in his diary (cf R. I. and S. Wilberforce, *The Life of William Wilberforce*, 1838, V, p.300). He wrote to Lawrence about some possible further days for sitting on 25 August of that year (R.A., MSS Law/5/266). Lawrence had received a first payment (of £78 15s.) for the portrait on 24 May. Probably what work was done on the picture was carried out in 1828. The picture was in Lawrence's studio at his death (Garlick, 1964, Appendix IV, no.281), noted as 'not ½ finished', and was claimed by Inglis.

The pose and composition were taken over by George Richmond in his pictures showing the sitter in an elaborate interior, and one at least of these was commissioned from him by Inglis.

*National Portrait Gallery, London*

## 50  Caroline, Duchess of Richmond (1796-1874)

Canvas, 254 × 160.1 (100 × 63)
*Provenance*: By family descent.
*Literature*: Garlick, 1954, p.55; 1964, p.168.

Caroline, eldest daughter of the 1st Marquess of Anglesey, married the future 5th Duke of Richmond in 1817; he succeeded his father as Duke in 1819.

Exhibited at the Academy in 1829 (no.102). Farington (*Diary*) recorded on 20 June 1821 a visit from Lawrence, who spoke of being 'pressed by applications to paint distinguished persons, viz. . . . The Duchess of Richmond'. A letter of earlier in the month, 5 June 1821, to Lawrence from the Duke of Richmond asked if the Duchess could see some of his pictures and if he would give her 'some sittings' (R.A., MSS Law/3/295). A reference by Lawrence himself in April 1829 (Williams, II, p.507) to being 'so hurried with the occupation of this season, and the getting ready two whole lengths', including this picture, suggests it was only then being finished, whenever begun.

Although Lawrence may have had no specific portrait by Van Dyck in mind, the echoes of his work in the composition and pose seem deliberate (and see under no.48). Christopher White has suggested orally that there is a derivation, in reverse, from the foreground figure of Lady Mary Villiers in Van Dyck's *Pembroke Family* (Wilton); she became Duchess of Richmond by her second marriage. Van Dyck and Stuart portrait-painters generally might seem particularly appropriate in painting a sitter whose title was Duchess of Richmond. A faint reminiscence of Ramsay's full-length of *Lady Mary Coke* in white (Marquess of Bute Collection), may be explained by a common indebtedness to Van Dyck.

The *Morning Advertiser* (5 May) thought Lawrence 'had thrown all his power of delineation and effect into the picture. Grace, elegance and symmetry unite . . .' The *Morning Journal* (2 May) found it the 'most attractive' of his exhibits: '. . . graceful and beautiful in the extreme . . . peculiarly happy in the landscape'. The *New Monthly Magazine* (1 June) also approved: 'the best of his female portraits'. The *Literary Gazette* (23 May) described it as 'manifestly resembling some of the portraits of Vandyke . . . and the result is a graceful and harmonious whole'. The *Athenaeum* (20 May) complained bitterly of the red curtain yet declared the picture 'pre eminent . . . a lovely subject, designed with the most courtly elegance, but with a slight dash of affectation'. The *Morning Chronicle* (14 May) thought it 'very beautiful' but 'an object of meaner note' between Wilkie's portrait of the Earl of Kellie and Pickersgill's *Jeremy Bentham*.

*The Trustees of the Goodwood Collections*

## 51   Selina, Lady Skipwith (1752–1832)

Canvas, 91.5 × 71.1 (36 × 28)
*Provenance*: Bequeathed by the sitter to the present owner's great-great-grandfather, Evelyn John Shirley.
*Literature*: Garlick, 1954, p.58; 1964, p.177.

Selina, eldest daughter of the Hon George Shirley, married Sir Thomas Skipwith, Bt, of Newbold Hall, Warwickshire, in 1785; he died in 1790. She was painted by Reynolds in 1787 (Frick Collection, New York).

Exhibited at the Birmingham Society for promoting the Fine Arts, 1829 (no.62). A letter of Lawrence's, of 2 February 1829, to his sister, Mrs Bloxam, living at Rugby, refers to a Lady 'Skipwill' (Williams, II, p.89), implying she is a neighbour and acquaintance of his sister's, and this must be a misprint for Skipwith. The present owner has kindly communicated a passage in a Memoir of the sitter, written by his great-grand-father, Evelyn Philip Shirley, the antiquarian and historian, recording that she was painted by Lawrence in June 1829 and that the picture was a gift to her from the artist, in return for her kindness to his sister: 'but Lady Skipwith had no idea of being thus indebted to Sir Thomas, and Mrs Bloxam received the £350 which he would otherwise have been paid'.

*Major John Shirley*

## 52   The 4th Earl of Aberdeen (1784-1860)

Canvas, 139.7 × 111.8 (55 × 44)
*Provenance*: Peel Heirlooms sale, London,
29 November 1917 (lot 89).
*Literature*: Garlick, 1954, p.23; 1964, p.14.

For the sitter, see no.24. He is shown wearing the star
and ribbon of the Thistle.

Exhibited at the Academy in 1830 (no.1), though the
picture is unfinished in places. It was commissioned
by (Sir) Robert Peel in the summer of 1829, when
Aberdeen was Foreign Secretary and Peel Home
Secretary in Wellington's Government. A letter of 5
August 1829 from Peel to Lawrence asks for Aberdeen
to be shown standing in the portrait, 'and as much after
the manner of Lord Durham's portrait as can properly
be' (R.A., MSS Law/5/260). Lawrence's half-length
portrait of Durham (previously J. G. Lambton; cf
no.42) had been shown at the Academy in 1829
(no.135) and is altogether a more 'private' image,
actually nearer Lawrence's earlier portrait of
Aberdeen, than the statesmanlike pose devised for the
present portrait. Lawrence wrote to Peel on 17 August
(Williams, II, p.513): 'I have seen Lord Aberdeen, who
comes to me on Wednesday'. He asked £262 10s. as
first half payment for the portrait.

Peel told his wife on 9 October 1829 that Lawrence
'has made a most beautiful head of Aberdeen for us'.

(*The Private Letters of Sir Robert Peel*, ed. G. Peel, 1920,
p.116.) A letter of 28 October from Lawrence to the
sitter (B.M., Add. MS 43234 f.39) speaks of the
satisfaction which 'your portrait has given to all your
friends who have seen it', making him less anxious for
that 'projected improvement of the lower part of the
face . . .'; and it proposes a short interval before the next
sitting.

Lawrence was represented posthumously at the
exhibition of 1830 by his usual number of eight
pictures. The *St James's Chronicle* (29 April-1 May)
thought the present portrait 'perhaps as fine a picture as
Lawrence ever produced'. The *Spectator* (8 May) gave a
long and favourable account of it: '. . . simple, natural
and unostentatious . . . gracefully composed and
beautifully painted . . . an air of courteous suavity
pervades the whole'. The *Athenaeum* (8 May) noted it
was unfinished but 'a beautiful picture'. The *Morning
Journal* (3 May) was 'disposed to think [it] the best' of
Lawrence's pictures exhibited. The *New Monthly
Magazine* (1 June) took, in effect, farewell of the artist
by saying: 'Had he painted no other portrait . . . it
would have immortalised him. It is identity, and what
is better it is the identity of an artist. The magic of his
art is thrown around the representations of the most
ordinary things, and, in his hands, the unpicturesque
costume of modern times – the coats and waistcoats of
modern man – lose their common place appearance'.

*The Viscount Cowdray*

# Drawings

**53a   Mrs, later Lady, Kenyon (1741-1808)**

Pencil on paper, 30.5 × 18.8 (12 × 7⅜)
Signed: *T. Lawrence/Fecit*
*Provenance*: By family descent.
*Literature*: Garlick, in *Burlington Magazine*, XCIII,
1951, p.253; 1964, p.232.

Lloyd Kenyon, barrister, became Attorney General in
1782 and Lord Chief Justice (1st Baron Kenyon) in
1788; he married in 1773 Mary, daughter of George
Kenyon of Peel Hall.
    Lawrence's earliest portrait drawings were in
profile, as here. The circumstances of the execution of
the present pair are described by Williams (I, pp.40-1):
they were done at the Black Bear Inn, Devizes, when it
was kept by Lawrence's father, and Mr and Mrs

**53b   Lloyd Kenyon, later 1st Baron Kenyon
(1732–1802)**

Pencil on paper, 30.5 × 18.8 (12 × 7⅜)
Signed: *T. Lawrence/Fecit*
For provenance, etc, see under no.53a

Kenyon stopped there. He gives the year as 1775 but it
seems in fact to have been only on 27 December 1779
that, according to Kenyon's diary, he and his wife
stayed at the Black Bear. These are among the earliest
surviving portrait drawings by Lawrence, though not
the very earliest; a profile of Charles Pepys (Garlick,
1964, p.240) is of 1777.

*The Lord Kenyon*

54

## 54 Self-portrait when a boy

Pencil on paper, 19 × 30.5 (7½ × 12)
*Provenance*: Inscribed on the mount as given to
Dr William Falconer (d.1824) of Bath, a very early
patron of Lawrence, with sixteen other drawings;
sold by J. H. Singer of Frome to J. F. Meehan of
Bath, 1900; Mary, Lady Newlands (d.1930); her
nephew, the 4th Marquess of Exeter.
*Literature*: Garlick, 1964, pp.232-3.

On the back is an inscription recording it as done by
Lawrence 'in Bath in 1786'. This date is anyway too
late, judging from Lawrence's appearance, though the
drawing was doubtless done at Bath (where the family
moved before the end of 1780). A smaller self-portrait
drawing (Garlick, loc. cit.), inscribed as done at the age
of twelve in 1781, offers close analogies, and Garlick
suggests that no.54 may be a rough sketch for it.

*The Marquess of Exeter*

## 55 Mrs Papendiek (1765-1839) with her son Frederick (1787-1811)

Red and black chalk on paper, 30.5 × 23.2 (12 × 9⅛)
Signed: *T. Lawrence/1789*
*Provenance*: Anonymous sale, Sotheby's 28 March
1924 (lot 3), bought C. Thomson; bequeathed by
George D. Pratt, 1935.
*Literature*: Garlick, 1964, p.239.

Charlotte Louisa Henrietta, daughter of Frederick
Albert, married Christopher Papendiek in 1783. She
became Assistant Keeper of the Wardrobe to Queen
Charlotte; her memoirs, *Court and Private Life in the
Time of Queen Charlotte*, were edited by Mrs V. Delves
Broughton, 1887.

Executed by Lawrence when at Windsor in the
autumn of 1789 to paint the full-length of the Queen
(no.3); Mrs Papendiek treated the young artist in a
notably friendly, helpful way. She herself recorded
(op. cit. II, pp.110-11) that she sat for the drawing in
the dress she had had new for the King's birthday, 4
June, and she also mentioned her bonnet (loc. cit.
p.129).

*Metropolitan Museum of Art, New York
(Bequest of George D. Pratt, 1935)*

## 56   Elizabeth Carter (1717–1806)

Chalks on paper, 31.1 × 27.3 (12¼ × 10¾)
*Provenance*: Lawrence sale, 18 June 1831 (lot 43),
bought Farrer.
*Literature*: Garlick, 1964, p.259.

The sitter was a miscellaneous and learned writer, a
poet, translator and a friend of Dr Johnson's.

Exhibited at the Academy in 1790 (no.145).
Lawrence had been active in the 1780s making portraits
in pastel, and he first exhibited at the Academy, in
1787, as a pastellist. After 1790 he largely ceased this
practice; the present picture was the only pastel he
exhibited in 1790, and his penultimate exhibit in the
medium.

On 5 May 1809 Farington received a letter from
Lawrence referring to an unfinished portrait he had of
the sitter which Farington could offer to Messrs Cadell
& Davies: a 'very strong likeness' of someone of
whom, Lawrence wrote, there had been no picture in
the latter part of her life (R.A., MSS Law/1/213).

The present portrait was engraved by C. Watson in
1806, presumably at the sitter's death.

*National Portrait Gallery, London*

## 57   Mrs Siddons (1755–1831)

Pencil on paper, 19 × 12.4 (7½ × 4¹³⁄₁₆)
*Provenance*: Lysons sale, Gloucester, 21 April 1887 (lot
322), bought Mrs W. E. Price; Mrs Alan Davidson
sale, London, 2 March 1976 (lot 142); both times as
'Emma Hamilton'.

Sarah, daughter of the actor Roger Kemble, married
the actor William Siddons in 1773. She became, and
has remained, the most famous English actress.
Lawrence drew and painted her on several occasions,
the first time at Bath in 1783. She and her daughters
became very friendly with him (cf no.67), with
complicated emotional results; but she and Lawrence
were reconciled before the end of their lives and she
intended him to be one of her pall-bearers.

The present drawing is unpublished in the literature
but was first brought to attention by Dr Kenneth
Garlick. It is the basis for an etching by Lawrence
himself, of which the British Museum impression is
inscribed: 'N.B. *This plate was etched as an experiment
which failed. T.L.*' (Garlick, 1964, p.243). It is in effect

55  *Mrs Papendiek with her son Frederick*

documented and dated by a letter of April 1830 from Daniel Lysons to Thomas Campbell which mentions the etching as done from 'the beautiful drawing of Mrs Siddons . . . before August 1790' (Williams, I, pp.101–2). An etching of an old woman (British Museum) is dated 1791.

Further confirmation of the period suggested by Lysons is provided by comparison of Mrs Siddons's costume with that of Mrs Papendick (no.55); Mrs Siddons wears a mob cap, for indoor wear, with the high crown that became fashionable for a few years about 1790, and the other indications of her dress accord with this date.

*Fine Arts Museums of San Francisco, Achenbach Foundation for Graphic Arts (Gift of the Goldyne Family in memory of Dr Alfred J. Goldyne, 1977.2.1)*

## 58  James Boswell (1740–95)

Pen on paper, 20.4 × 16.2 (8 × 6$\frac{3}{8}$)
*Provenance*: By family descent.
*Literature*: J. Kerslake, *Mr Boswell* (National Portrait Gallery exhibition catalogue), 1967, no.101.

The sitter, biographer of Dr Johnson, was Secretary for Foreign Correspondence at the Royal Academy from 1791.

The present sketch vaguely relates to a semi-caricature profile sketch of Boswell done by Lawrence at about the same period, that is in Boswell's last years, and which exists in several versions (cf Garlick, 1964, p.217). It is tempting to suggest that they date from 1791, the year in which Lawrence became ARA and Boswell the Secretary for Foreign Correspondence. The caricature element is more forceful in the present sketch and, even allowing for this, Boswell's appearance seems to have deteriorated. Kerslake, loc. cit., appositely quotes Farington (*Diary*, 6 October 1793): 'met Boswell, who I think is much altered for the worse in appearance'.

*A naval descendant of close friends of Sir Thomas Lawrence*

## 59  Emilia Mary Boucherett (1790–1874) with a doll

Red and black chalk on paper, 25 × 18 (9$\frac{7}{8}$ × 7$\frac{1}{8}$)
Signed: *TL/1793*
*Provenance*: By family descent.
*Literature*: Garlick, 1964, p.217; Garlick, in *Burlington Magazine*, CX, 1968, p.674.

Emilia Mary was the eldest daughter of Ayscoghe Boucherett, MP, of Willingham Hall, Lincolnshire, and Emily, née Crockett, daughter of the first Mrs John Julius Angerstein by her first marriage. She died unmarried. Lawrence made other drawings of her, her mother and her siblings, as well as painting a portrait of her with her brother Ayscoghe Junior. He showed a *Portrait of Mr Boucherett's Children* at the Academy in 1800. Mrs Boucherett was one of Lawrence's closest friends.

*Colonel Michael E. St J. Barne*

## 60  A private concert

Red and black chalk on paper, 45.7 × 45 (18 × 17$\frac{3}{4}$)
Signed (in the hat): *TL is at*
*Provenance*: Mrs G. Salusbury Hughes sale, London, 20 March 1957 (lot 114).
*Literature*: Garlick, 1964, p.254.

A long inscription, written by John Hughes in 1832 and originally pasted on the backboard, identifies the scene as at Mr Blencowe's of Hayes: '. . . the gentleman fiddling was Peter Denys who married Lady Charlotte Fermor', and states that Lawrence went with the Hughes family to one of Blencowe's concerts in 1796 and sent John Hughes's father the drawing the next day. In fact, Farington (*Diary*, ed. K. Garlick and A. Macintyre, II, 1978, p.364) records on 11 July 1795 breakfasting with Hughes: 'Lawrence has made an excellent drawing of certain characters who attend Mr Blencowes concert [sic]. – Blencowe & his man, – Peter Denyss, & a Lady at the Harpischord'.

*Kenneth Garlick*

59

60

58

61   *Richard Westall*

## 61 Richard Westall (1765-1836)

Black chalk on paper, 18 × 22.9 (7 × 9)
Signed or inscribed: *T. Lawrence.. R. Westall del.*
*Provenance*: An inscription pasted on the back, and
dating from 1918, records the drawing as given by
the sitter's brother, William Westall (d.1850), to his
niece Miss Daniell, daughter of the artist William
Daniell (1769-1837).

The sitter, historical painter and prolific draughtsman,
RA, 1794, was a close friend of Lawrence's in his early
years in London and lodged for a time at 57 Greek
Street, where Lawrence and his parents lived.
    The present drawing is unpublished. Owing to
misinterpretation of the wording on it, it has passed for
many years as a drawing of Lawrence by Westall, but
there can be no doubt that the sitter is Westall. The
striking physiognomy may best be compared with
Westall's own self-portrait of 1793 (Royal Academy),
which is presumably the picture he exhibited at the
Academy in 1794 (no.111). The date of the present
drawing is likely to be of no later than the mid 1790s.

*Private collection*

## 62 Henry Fuseli (1741-1825)

Pencil on paper, 27.3 × 19.4 ($10\frac{3}{4}$ × $7\frac{5}{8}$)
*Provenance*: W. Benoni White; C. Fairfax Murray,
from whom purchased, 1890.
*Literature*: Garlick, 1964, p.227.

The sitter (properly Johann Heinrich Füssli), painter
and writer, RA, 1790, was a friend of Lawrence's;
Lawrence admired his imaginative power (and cf
no.63), and Fuseli – though not uncritical – could be a
perceptive admirer of Lawrence's work.
    The drawing must date from no later than 1796,
when it was engraved by T. Holloway. There is
otherwise little indication of the date of its execution;
Garlick, loc. cit., proposes *c.*1795. Williams (I, p.133)
mentions that Lawrence was asked to draw a portrait
of Fuseli for the English edition of Lavater's
*Physiognomische Fragmente*, which was published in
1792.

*The Trustees of the British Museum*

## 63   Satan as a fallen angel

Pencil and water colour on paper, 24.7 × 20.4
($9\frac{3}{4}$ × 8)
*Provenance*: By family descent; possibly given by the
artist to Mrs Boucherett.
*Literature*: Garlick, 1964, p.255.

In 1797 Lawrence exhibited at the Academy his large-
scale *Satan summoning his legions* (Royal Academy),
illustrating Milton's *Paradise Lost*, Book I, ll. 300 ff, an
attempt at the grand and sublime, influenced by Fuseli
among others, which was not well received.

   Some studies for the picture exist, but the present
drawing seems unlikely to be a preparatory work. It is
unrelated in composition, as well as highly finished,
and may seem rather to be an offshoot of his thinking
around the subject, probably at about the same date.
That Lawrence continued to think about the subject is
revealed by an undated letter of possibly around 1804
(Williams, II, p.49), in which he exclaims: 'I would
rather paint Satan, bursting into tears, when collecting
his ruined angels, than Achilles, radiant in his heavenly
arms . . . rushing on devoted Troy!'

   In this drawing the moment depicted is probably
not that of Satan summoning his legions but of his
earlier awakening, with Beelzebub beside him, to the
fiery horror of hell and expressing his defiance of the
Almighty:
>      With head uplift above the wave, and eyes
>      That sparkling blazed;
Satan's appearance seems to take account of the later
lines (591-3):
>          His form had yet not lost
>      All her original brightness, nor appeared
>      Less than Archangel ruined,
A version exists in a private collection.

*Colonel Michael E. St J. Barne*

## 64 Meadows opposite Sloane Street

Black and white chalk on blue-grey paper,
$28.5 \times 28.5$ ($11\frac{1}{4} \times 11\frac{1}{4}$)
*Provenance*: William Hamilton, R A, posthumous sale,
London, 10 May, 1802 (lot 221); W. Esdaile (d.1837);
Matthew Hutchinson sale, London, 22 February 1861
(lot 101); purchased from a Mr Jackson, 1885.
*Literature*: Garlick, 1964, p.253.

The drawing must anyway date from pre-1801, when
Hamilton, a close friend of Lawrence's, died, and is
probably of the 1790s. On the reverse a label signed by
Esdaile records that on showing the drawing to
Lawrence: 'when spending the day with me at my
house on Clapham Common the 31 October 1829, he
acknowledged it to be a genuine portraiture of the
meadows opposite to Sloane Street before they were
built upon, and which he drew from recollection after
returning home one moonlight night'.

The reference to the 'meadows opposite Sloane
Street' does not unfortunately help in dating the
drawing, since on a map as late as 1804 the site of
Belgravia, between Sloane Street and Grosvenor Place,
is shown as still covered with fields. Lawrence's
response to, and sustained interest in, landscape could
be deduced from the backgrounds especially to his
early portraits, in addition to his comments in letters. A
comparable chalk study, of a *Pool with trees*, exists
(Garlick, loc. cit.), and two oil sketches of landscapes
by him are known.

*The Trustees of the British Museum*

**66    William Lock (1732-1810) and his daughter
Amelia (1771-1848)**

Black and red chalk on paper, 29.8 × 24.1 (11¾ × 9½)
*Provenance*: By family descent.
*Literature*: Garlick, 1964, pp.234-5; Garlick, in
*Burlington Magazine*, CX, 1968, p.670.

William Lock of Norbury Park, collector and
connoisseur, was one of Lawrence's earliest patrons
after coming to London; Lawrence exhibited a portrait
of him at the Academy in 1790 (no.19), and a portrait
of his widow at the Academy in 1829 (no.455), in
addition to making other paintings and drawings of
members of the family. His daughter Amelia married
John Angerstein in 1799 (cf no.74).

On the portfolio beside Lock the initials: *WL*.

Garlick, loc. cit. 1968, mentions Lock's valetudinarian ways and points out how close the depiction is
to a passage in Farington (*Diary*, 12 July 1796; ed. K.
Garlick and A. Macintyre, II, 1978, p.604), describing
Lock: 'He seldom goes out of the House, and
complains of cold feet, in so much so, that He sits on
thick carpet & close to the fire, at this Season.' The
drawing is anyway likely to date from before Amelia
Lock's marriage in 1799 and may well be from around
1796. The portfolio might be of prints collected by
Lock or conceivably of the work of his son William
Lock II, a talented draughtsman.

*Colonel Michael E. St J. Barne*

**65    Nude torso of a man, and a knee**

Black chalk on brown paper, heightened with white,
25.4 × 17.5 (10 × 6⅞)
*Provenance*: Bequeathed by Alexander Dyce, 1869.
*Literature*: Garlick, 1964, p.255.

This and another very similar study of a man's leg (also
Dyce bequest) are rare surviving examples of academy
studies by Lawrence. They are dated by Garlick to the
1790s and seem to be done from the life, possibly at the
Academy Schools, which Lawrence attended for a
period from September 1787. Henry Howard, RA,
later told Williams (I, p.99): 'His proficiency in
drawing, even at that time, was such as to leave all his
competitors in the antique school far behind him.'

*Victoria and Albert Museum*

**67 Cecilia and Sally (?) Siddons**

Pencil on paper, 19 × 14 (7½ × 5½)
*Provenance*: Possibly Lysons sale, Gloucester, 21 April
1887 (lot 319): 'Miss Siddons and Miss Cecilia
Siddons'.
*Literature*: Garlick, 1964, p.244.

Cecilia Siddons (1794-1868) was the fifth daughter of
Mrs Siddons (cf no.57); she married George Combe in
1833. Sally (Sarah Martha) Siddons (1775-1803) was
the eldest daughter; Lawrence was, unofficially at least,
engaged to her, but became involved with her sister
Maria (1779-98), who on her deathbed made Sally
promise never to marry Lawrence.

Judging from Cecilia Siddons's appearance, the
drawing must date from around 1797. The identity of
the profile head is not easily resolved, because Sally
and Maria Siddons looked very similar; however,
Lawrence's profile drawings of Sally, one of them
identified in his own handwriting ('This drawing is
Miss Siddons'), suggest that it is she who is shown here.
If the present drawing is that from the Lysons sale (and
no other drawing of the two sisters together is known),
there seems to be additional confirmation that the
identification is correct.

*Private collection*

**68 Julia Angerstein, later Mme Sabloukoff
(1772-1846)**

Pencil, red chalk and wash on paper, 24.5 × 22.2
(9⅝ × 8¾)
*Provenance*: Bequeathed by Miss May Rowley (a
descendant of John Julius Angerstein) to Mrs Ralph
Oliphant, 1965; Mrs Oliphant sale, Sotheby's
23 November 1967 (lot 40); Mr and Mrs Cyril Fry.
*Literature*: Garlick, in *Burlington Magazine*, CX, 1968,
p.674.

The sitter, more properly Juliana, was the daughter of
John Julius Angerstein (cf no.7) by his first marriage;
she married General Nikolai Sabloukoff (1776-1848)
on 20 November 1804, against her father's wishes, but
they were later reconciled. The couple settled in Russia
in 1807.

Lawrence drew and painted her on other occasions,
and also painted a portrait of her husband. Garlick, loc.
cit., suggested a date of probably *c*.1800 when
publishing this drawing. The costume indications,
including the jewellery, would place the drawing
somewhere between approximately 1797 and 1802.

*Sir John R. H. Thouron, KBE*

## 69 Isabel Smith

Pencil and red chalk on card, 35.5 × 30.25
(14 × 11$\frac{15}{16}$)
*Provenance*: Bequeathed by Miss May Rowley (a descendant of John Julius Angerstein) to the National Gallery, and transferred, 1965.
*Literature*: *The Tate Gallery Report 1965–66*, p.18.

The sitter was apparently a nurse in the Angerstein family and known as Munia. Inscribed on the reverse is her identity: '... my Nurse Isabel Smith, called Munia, buried at N[h] Willingham Lincoln[e]. W[m] Angerstein,

drawn by S[r] Tho[s] Lawrence at Woodlands'. William Angerstein, youngest grandson of John Julius Angerstein, was not born until 1812; Woodlands was the family villa at Blackheath. Willingham Hall was the home of Mr and Mrs Ayscoghe Boucherett (cf no.59).

Two repetitions of the drawing exist (one amid the R.A. Lawrence MS material). For those, Garlick (1964, p.244) has proposed a date of *c*.1800, but presumably the drawing could be rather later.

*The Trustees of the Tate Gallery*

## 70 Lady Frances Hamilton, later Countess of Wicklow (1792–1860)

Red and black chalk on paper, 54.9 × 32.4
(21⅝ × 12¾)
Signed: *T.L. Feb (?) 1804*
*Provenance*: Bequeathed by Anne, Lady Milford (the sitter's daughter), to Sir William Baillie Hamilton, 1909; Major W. S. Baillie-Hamilton sale, Sotheby's 18 November 1953 (lot 121), bought Leggatt; later with Spink & Son.
*Literature*: Garlick, 1964, p.229.

The sitter was the fourth daughter of the 1st Marquess of Abercorn and only child of his second marriage; she married the 3rd Earl of Wicklow in 1816.

Further for Lawrence's friendship with and work for the Marquess of Abercorn, see no.22.

*Mrs Montagnie Van Norden*

## 71 The Allnutt family

Red and black chalk on paper, 50.5 × 35.5
(19⅞ × 14)
*Provenance*: Agnew's, *105th Annual Exhibition of Watercolours and Drawings*, 1978 (no.175).
*Literature*: Garlick, 1964, p.211.

John Allnutt (*c*.1774–1863) was painted by Lawrence in a full-length portrait (no.13); his first wife was Elizabeth, daughter of John Douce Garthwaite, who died in 1810. Their daughter was Anna (1801–28).

From an old photograph the drawing was dated *c*.1805 by Garlick, loc. cit., but this seems too late for the age of the child; no later than 1803 would appear more likely. Lawrence drew and painted Mrs Allnutt (R.A., 1798 (no.30)); to the latter portrait Anna Allnutt was added *c*.1803.

*J. M. Alabaster, Esq*

**72 Mrs Charles Wall (c.1768–1838)**

Red and black chalk on paper, 21.6 × 17.8 (8½ × 7)
*Provenance*: J. Pierpont Morgan sale, Christie's
31 March 1944 (lot 101), bought Agnew's.
*Literature*: Garlick, 1964, p.213.

Harriet, eldest daughter of Sir Francis Baring, Bt,
married Charles Wall in 1790 (for her father and her
husband, see no.23). Her death, 'in her 70th year', is
noted in the *Gentleman's Magazine* on 5 March 1838.

Lawrence exhibited at the Academy in 1810
(no.159) a group portrait of (Sir) Thomas Baring and
his wife with their son Francis Thornhill Baring (no.73
here), and Mrs Wall, Sir Thomas's sister, with her son
Charles Baring Wall. In late 1807 and again in late 1808
he was staying at Sir Francis Baring's, executing
various portraits; they were in 1808 to include
paintings of two of Sir Francis's grandchildren but,
owing to measles in the house, these were not executed
(R.A., MSS Law/2/202).

On these visits Lawrence executed some drawings of
members of the family. The present drawing is a study
in its own right but the sitter's appearance is fairly close
to that in the group portrait of 1810. Garlick dates the
drawing to *c.* 1805–10, with a query. It certainly seems
of no later than 1810, and the period 1807–8 may
reasonably be proposed.

*Baring Brothers & Company Ltd*

**73 Francis Thornhill Baring, later 1st Baron Northbrook (1796–1866)**

Black and red chalk on paper 21.6 × 17.2 (8½ × 6¾)
Signed (under the sitter's left arm): *T.L./1807/1811*
*Provenance*: J. Pierpont Morgan sale, Christie's
31 March 1944 (lot 100), bought Agnew's.
*Literature*: Garlick, 1964, p.213.

The sitter, eldest son of Sir Thomas Baring, 2nd Bt,
and grandson of Sir Francis Baring, 1st Bt, held various
high Government offices; he was created Baron
Northbrook in 1866.

The drawing must date basically from 1807 and
record the sitter's appearance at that time. Lawrence
was staying at Sir Francis Baring's Hampshire house in
November 1807. The sitter appears differently posed
but not significantly older in the Baring family group
with his parents, aunt and cousin, which Lawrence
exhibited in 1810; an oil study for the sitter's head in
that picture exists. After the exhibition of the group
portrait Lawrence may have slightly worked up the
present drawing, especially in the head, and possibly
given it to a member of the Baring family.

*Baring Brothers & Company Ltd*

**74 Mrs John Angerstein (1771-1848) nursing a child**

Red and black chalk on paper, 40.1 × 26.2 (16 × 10½)
Inscribed on the back: *Willingham 1810*
*Provenance*: By family descent.
*Literature*: Garlick, 1964, p.212.

For the sitter, née Amelia Lock, see no.66; she is nursing probably her fourth child, Frederick, born in 1809.

The drawing was executed at Willingham Hall, Lincolnshire, the home of Mr and Mrs Ayscoghe Boucherett; Mrs Boucherett was the daughter of John Julius Angerstein's first wife by her first marriage (cf no.59). Probably on the same visit, and certainly in the same year, Lawrence also drew a composite portrait with the head based on the present sitter and the body on Mrs Boucherett.

*Private collection*

## 75　Mrs George Stratton (c.1778-1861)

Black and coloured chalks on canvas, 91.5 × 78.7
(36 × 31)
*Provenance*: By family descent to Bevil Granville,
from whom purchased, 1954.
*Literature*: Garlick, 1964, p.245.

For the sitter, see no.25.

Apparently cut down from a full-length, in which
case it has been drastically reduced all round to judge
from the proportions of the completed full-length
portrait of the sitter also exhibited here.

The work must date from around 1810 when Mrs
Stratton was sitting to Lawrence. Although the pose in
the drawing differs from that in the painted portrait,
the angle of the head and the sitter's general appearance
are similar enough to suggest that both likenesses were
taken at the same period. Garlick (in R.A., *Lawrence*
exhibition catalogue, 1961, under no.83) makes the
point that, while Lawrence's practice was to draw the
figure carefully on canvas before he began to paint, this
is the only recorded example of a full-length not
painted on at all. Lady Elizabeth Leveson-Gower's
comments on Lawrence's portraits at this stage of
execution may be recalled (see under no.34).

An oval painting, also at Birmingham, seems to be
based on the present drawing. Although accepted in
the literature as originally full length, the drawing as it
stands composes so well as to suggest it may have been
conceived in its present format.

*City Museums and Art Gallery, Birmingham*

## 76　The Duchess of Wellington (1773-1831)

Red and black chalk on paper, 29.8 × 21.9
($11\frac{3}{4}$ × $8\frac{5}{8}$)
Signed: *TL. 1814*
*Provenance*: Executed for the Hon Mrs Henry
Hamilton (d.1854), the Duchess's sister, by whom
given or bequeathed to the 2nd Duke of Wellington.
*Literature*: Garlick, 1964, p.247.

The sitter, the Hon Catherine Pakenham, married the
future 1st Duke of Wellington in 1806.

The Duke of Wellington sat to Lawrence in July
1814 for a full-length portrait, and it may have been
about this period – while London was celebrating his
victories – that the Duchess sat for the present drawing.
Without indicating the date, Miss Croft records
meeting at Lawrence's the Duchess of Wellington
(Layard, p.258), and repeats an anecdote about the
Duke's mother which the Duchess told Lawrence at a
sitting (loc. cit. p.261). When the Duchess had sat to
some artist for a portrait in 1810 her friend Maria
Edgeworth had commented: 'it is absurd to draw Lady
Wellington's face; she has no *face*, it is all countenance'
(quoted in E. Longford, *Wellington, the years of the
sword*, 1971 edn, p.290).

The Duchess wrote to Lawrence in 1822 begging
him to complete a portrait of the Duke for the library
at Stratfield Saye. In 1827 Lawrence executed and
presented to her a pencil drawing he had done of her
elder son, the future 2nd Duke.

*The Duke of Wellington*

76   *The Duchess of Wellington*

## 77  Lady Bagot, Lady Fitzroy Somerset, later Lady Raglan, and Lady Burghersh, later Countess of Westmorland

Red and black chalk on paper, 60.9 × 53.3 (24 × 21)
Signed: *TL 1814*
*Provenance*: By family descent.
*Literature*: Garlick, 1964, pp.218–19.

The sitters were daughters of the 3rd Earl of Mornington, an elder brother of Wellington's. Mary Charlotte Anne (d.1845) married in 1806 Sir Charles Bagot; Emily Harriet (1792–1881) married in 1814 Lord Fitzroy Somerset, later 1st Baron Raglan; Priscilla Anne (1793–1879) had married in 1811 Lord Burghersh, later 11th Earl of Westmorland.

As the central figure is Emily Harriet, who was married on 6 August 1814 in London, it may be that the drawing relates to this event when the sisters were presumably united. Alternatively, it is conceivable that the drawing was done in Paris after the entry of the Allies at the end of March, when Lawrence briefly visited the city. Sir Charles Bagot and Lord Fitzroy Somerset were there; Lady Burghersh accompanied her husband to Paris at the same period but by 1815 seems to have been with him in Florence. A letter from her to Lawrence, written from Paris in October 1814 (Layard, p.103), shows an interest in his art and willingness to see examples of it displayed in the British Embassy there while Wellington was ambassador.

The composition vaguely suggests, apparently without copying any prototype, pictorial treatments of the Three Graces and the Three Fates, the latter of whom are sometimes shown seated on the ground.

A replica, unsigned and undated, is in the collection of the Duke of Wellington. Garlick lists several repetitions of the heads only.

*Private collection*

## 78 Antonio Canova (1757-1822)

Red, black and white chalk on brown paper,
54.6 × 55.8 (21½ × 22)
*Provenance*: Perhaps '. . . the original cartoon
presented by the artist to one of the family',
anonymous sale, Foster, 23 April 1902 (lot 102),
bought Rolls; possibly the same item in anonymous
sales in 1923 and 1958; anonymous sale, Sotheby's
27 October 1961 (lot 11), bought Maggs.
*Literature*: Garlick, 1964, p.220.

The famous Italian sculptor visited England in the
autumn of 1815, partly to see the Elgin marbles. He
was very well received in society and by artists, and
became friendly with Lawrence. The Prince Regent
commissioned a portrait of Canova from Lawrence
and presented it to the sitter (R.A., 1816 (no.184), now
in the Gipsoteca, Possagno).

   Canova is posed very similarly in the Possagno
painting (of which a large number of replicas exist) and
in the present drawing, but he is more formally dressed
in the drawing and appears altogether less consciously
presented as an artist. The drawing might all the same
be the basis for the painting, recording Canova's
appearance as he actually first sat when in London.

   In the Lawrence sale of 19 June 1830 (lot 407) was a
drawing of Canova in red, black and white chalks, of
the same dimensions as the present drawing, but said to
be on canvas.

*John Goelet*

## 79 Samuel Rogers (1763-1855)

Red and black chalk on paper, 29.8 × 21.9
(11¾ × 8⅝)
*Provenance*: Bequeathed by Henry Vaughan, 1900.
*Literature*: Garlick, 1964, p.241.

The sitter, banker, versifier and social figure, knew
Lawrence quite well but commented to Farington
(*Diary*, 7 June 1818) about his being 'a very reserved
character . . .'

   A painted portrait of him was claimed at Lawrence's
death by Miss Rogers but was noted as 'not found'. At
the same time a drawing of him ('Do in crayons') was
found and handed over to her and that is probably the
drawing now in the National Portrait Gallery,
presented by H. Rogers in 1875; it is dated by Garlick
to *c*.1825, with a query. The present drawing would
seem to be earlier; Garlick dates it with a query to
*c*.1815, and notes it was engraved in or by 1822.

*The Trustees of the British Museum*

80   *Sir Richard Croft, Bt*

## 80 Sir Richard Croft, Bt (1762-1818)

Black and red chalk on paper, 37.4 × 25.4
($14\frac{3}{4}$ × 10)
*Provenance*: By family descent.
*Literature*: Garlick, 1964, p.223.

The sitter, the 6th Baronet, accoucheur, was accused of negligence following the death in 1817 of Princess Charlotte, after giving birth to a still-born son, and shot himself; his sister, Elizabeth Croft, was a close friend of Lawrence's (see further below).

Lawrence had executed a drawing of Sir Richard Croft, *c*.1810. Croft committed suicide on 13 February 1818, while attending a childbed that apparently recalled Princess Charlotte's.

Shortly afterwards, Lawrence made for Miss Croft the present drawing of him in his coffin. She refers to it in her Recollections (Layard, pp.244-5): 'by his magical power [he] contrived to give it the appearance of sleep in his armchair'. According to her testimony, Lawrence considered it one of his most exquisite performances and it was called by one friend 'the triumph of Genius over death', and warmly praised by Wilkie.

*Richard Page Croft, Esq*

## 81 Countess Rosalie Rzewuska (1788-1865)

Black chalk with touches of water colour on paper,
41.3 × 26.4 ($16\frac{5}{16}$ × $10\frac{7}{16}$)
*Provenance*: Lent by Miss Croft to the British Institution, 1830 (no.64); Lawrence sale, London, 18 June 1831 (A5), bought Woodburn; purchased by the British Museum, 1900.
*Literature*: Garlick, 1964, p.242; *Portrait Drawings*, British Museum exhibition, 1964, no.313.

The sitter, born Princess Rosalie Lubomirska, married her cousin Wenzel, Graf Rzewuski, in 1808. He was of a famous Polish family but had been brought up in Vienna and had served in the Austrian army under the Archduke Charles (cf no.37).

A label formerly on the drawing stated that Lawrence executed the drawing in Vienna. It was presumably among the drawings he did there in the early months of 1819, and he himself lists it in a letter of 19 May 1819 (Williams, II, p.146). What is not clear is why it remained with him.

*The Trustees of the British Museum*

## 82   An Uhlan Orderly with a horse

Pencil on paper, 49.9 × 40 (19$\frac{11}{16}$ × 15$\frac{13}{16}$)
*Provenance*: Lawrence sale, London, 18 June 1831 (lot
119); Alpine Gallery, London, 1955 (no.19), whence
purchased.
*Literature*: Garlick, 1964, p.242.

At the right numerous colour notes by the artist for the
uniform.

The drawing is a careful study for the subsidiary but
quite prominent figure and horse in Lawrence's
portrait of Prince Schwarzenberg, Austrian Field-
Marshal and Commander-in-Chief, which is one of
the Waterloo Chamber series (Millar, no.912).
Lawrence seems to have been working on the picture
in Vienna at the end of 1818 and early in 1819.

The present width of the portrait is almost two feet
larger than Lawrence's standard canvas for full-lengths
in this series, and Millar indicates that the canvas has
been enlarged during painting to include the Uhlan
and horse. The Uhlan must be a portrait and he was
presumably included at Schwarzenberg's wish. The
pose of the horse is virtually the same as that in
Lawrence's portrait of the Cossack general, Count
Platov (Millar, no.910), which had been painted in
London in 1814.

*The Visitors of the Ashmolean Museum, Oxford*

## 83   Cardinal Ercole Consalvi (1757-1824)

Black and red chalk on paper, 38.7 × 27.3 (15$\frac{1}{4}$ × 10$\frac{3}{4}$)
*Provenance*: Given by the artist to Elizabeth, Duchess of
Devonshire, by whom bequeathed to her brother, 1st
Marquess of Bristol, 1824.
*Literature*: Garlick, 1964, p.222.

The sitter became the close adviser and chief minister
of Pope Pius VII (cf no.38).

Executed in Rome in 1819 when Lawrence was
painting the full-length portraits of Consalvi and the
Pope. According to Cardinal Wiseman (*Recollections of
the last four Popes*, 1858, p.27), Consalvi had never
previously agreed to sit for his portrait. Lawrence
described his physiognomy as 'full of sagacity and
energy' (Williams, II, p.186).

The drawing closely accords with the pose and
appearance of Consalvi in the painted portrait (Millar,
no.893) and must be based on this. Such a procedure is
unusual with Lawrence but is explained by the
circumstances. The Duchess of Devonshire (cf no.21)
was a friend and great admirer of Consalvi. A letter of
hers to Lawrence, dated 3 September 1819 (Layard,

p.152) begs him 'Not to forget your kind promise to me of leaving a drawing with me of that inimitable picture . . .' This reference must be to the portrait of Consalvi. Lawrence left Rome in December 1819. The Duchess mentions the drawing in her will of 1821, stating that the sitter's 'constant kindness makes Rome delightful to me' (quoted by D. M. Stuart, *Dearest Bess*, 1955, p.240).

The drawing was with Lawrence at his death (Garlick, Appendix IV, nos.2 and 161), having been lent to him presumably for the lithograph (of 1830) by F. C. Lewis.

*The National Trust, Ickworth*

## 84    George IV

Black, red and white chalk on brownish paper,
91.5 × 76.2 (36 × 30)
*Provenance*: Possibly the oval drawing in the
Lawrence sale, London, 18 June 1831 (lot 131),
bought Lord Chesterfield and so presumably the oval
'from Bretby Hall', anonymous sale, Christie's
21 January 1927 (lot 3), bought Harrison.

For the sitter, see under no.33.

The present drawing is unpublished; it was kindly brought to attention by Sir Oliver Millar. Garlick, 1964, p.228, records the existence of an oval drawing with the provenance above.

There are pentimenti in the outline of the shoulders and coat collar.

The drawing relates to the painted portrait of the King in private dress for which he was sitting in 1822 (cf fig.3) and of which there are numerous replicas, some half-length and one at least head and bust only (cf Garlick, 1964, pp.87-8). The drawing differs from the painting in seeming not to show the King in a fur-collared coat, as well as omitting his decorations. Lawrence described the original full-length portrait as 'perhaps my most successful resemblance (of the King), and the most interesting from its being so entirely of a simple domestic nature' (Williams, II, p.319).

*Her Majesty Queen Elizabeth, The Queen Mother*

84

85

## 85 Prince George of Cumberland, later King George V of Hanover (1819-78)

Black, red and white chalk on canvas, 60 × 42 ($23\frac{11}{16}$ × $16\frac{9}{16}$)
*Provenance*: Lawrence sale, London, 19 June 1830 (lot 417), bought Moon; presented to the sitter by F. G. Moon, 1843.
*Literature*: Garlick, 1964, p.223.

The sitter, grandson of George III and son of Ernest, Duke of Cumberland, succeeded his father as King of Hanover in 1851. He visited England with his parents in the spring of 1828, when Lady Holland described him as '. . . a lively, pretty boy; & if he says half the witty things attributed to him, he must be a remarkable child' (*Elizabeth, Lady Holland to her son*, ed. Earl of Ilchester, 1946, p.83).

A letter of George IV's to the sitter's father (quoted in C. Hibbert, *George IV*, 1976 edn, p.739) anticipates the family's visit and mentions ' my beloved George'. The Cumberland visit lasted until August of 1828.

An undated letter to Lawrence from (Sir) Frederick Watson, the King's Assistant Private Secretary, records having just returned from Windsor and the King's wish that Lawrence should paint Prince George (R.A., MSS Law/5/242). The present drawing is likely to have been Lawrence's preliminary study for the full-length portrait in the Royal Collection (Millar, no.882); in the painting the sitter looks away from the spectator and his hair has a neater appearance.

According to Williams (II, p.490), the portrait was painted at Cumberland Lodge, where Lawrence stayed 'for the purpose for six weeks'; but it was still unfinished in his studio at his death.

*HRH The Prince of Hanover*

## 86 William Hyde Wollaston (1766-1828)

Black and red chalk on paper, 33 × 23.5 (13 × $9\frac{1}{4}$)
Signed: *T.L. P.R.A./October 1828*
*Provenance*: Given by the artist to the 2nd Earl Spencer.
*Literature*: Garlick, 1964, p.250.

The sitter, a distinguished chemist and physicist, was friendly with Lawrence; he published in 1824 a paper on the direction of the eyes, illustrated by one of Lawrence's portraits.

Wollaston had been conscious of being gravely ill since the end of 1827. In an undated letter to Lawrence (R.A., MSS Law/5/267), probably of the summer or early autumn 1828, he agreed to sit, 'in all feebleness', for what must be the present drawing. He died on 22 December that year. After his death the family declined the work and regretted its 'failure' because it was undertaken when Wollaston was ill (R.A., MSS Law/5/310). Lawrence was told he was free to dispose of it, and he gave it to Lord Spencer.

It was in Lawrence's studio at his death (Garlick, Appendix IV, no.237), presumably in connection with the lithograph of 1830 by F. C. Lewis, and was claimed by Lord Spencer. In the Lawrence sale, Christie's 17 June 1830, lot 456 was the Lewis lithograph noted as not published.

Earlier portraits of Wollaston include two by John Jackson, RA.

*Earl Spencer*

86   *William Hyde Wollaston*

88   *John Abernethy*

## 87   Countess Grey and her daughters

*Literature*: Garlick, 1964, pp.95-6.

Mary Elizabeth Ponsonby (1776-1831), daughter of the 1st Lord Ponsonby, married the Hon Charles Grey, son of the 1st Earl Grey (cf no.11), in 1794. The children shown are probably Caroline (d.1875) and Georgiana (1801-1900).

The original portrait was begun in 1805. This engraving by S. Cousins (1801-87) was published in 1831.

*Private collection*

## 89   Lady Peel (1795-1859)

*Literature*: Garlick, 1964, p.159.

Julia, youngest daughter of General Sir John Floyd, married the future Sir Robert Peel, 2nd Bt, in 1820. She, her husband and their eldest daughter all sat to Lawrence for portraits during the 1820s.

The original portrait (cf fig.4) was exhibited at the Academy in 1827 (no.134). This engraving by Cousins was published in 1832.

*Private collection*

## 88   John Abernethy (1764–1831)

*Literature*: Garlick, 1964, p.15.

The sitter was a Fellow of the Royal Society and surgeon at St Bartholomew's hospital.

The original portrait was exhibited at the Academy in 1820 (no.115). This engraving by W. Bromley (1769-1842) was published in 1827.

*Private collection*

# LIST OF LENDERS

Her Majesty The Queen    19, 35, 37, 38, 43

Her Majesty Queen Elizabeth, The Queen Mother    84

HRH The Prince of Hanover    85

The Duke of Abercorn    9, 22

J. M. Alabaster, Esq    71

Sir Philip Antrobus, Bt    18

The Visitors of the Ashmolean Museum, Oxford    82

Baring Brothers & Company Ltd    23, 39, 72, 73

Colonel Michael E. St J. Barne    59, 63, 66

The Earl Bathurst    5

City Museums and Art Gallery, Birmingham    75

The Trustees of the British Museum    62, 64, 79, 81

The Trustees of the Chatsworth Settlement    8

The Art Institute of Chicago    29

The Viscount Cowdray    52

Richard Page Croft, Esq    80

The City of Dublin    33

The Lord Bishop of Durham and the Church Commissioners for England    31

Tom Egerton, Esq    13

The Marquess of Exeter    54

Sir Andrew G. Forbes-Leith, Bt    2

Kenneth Garlick    60

John Goelet    78

The Trustees of the Goodwood Collections    50

Earl Granville    20

Guildhall Art Gallery    12

The Principal and Fellows of Jesus College, Oxford    47

The Lord Kenyon    53a and b

Lord Lambton    42

The Marquess of Londonderry    28, 48

Los Angeles County Museum of Art    6

Musée du Louvre    7

Metropolitan Museum of Art, New York    4, 41, 55

The Trustees of the National Gallery    3

National Gallery of Art, Washington    17

National Gallery of Ireland, Dublin    21

National Gallery of Scotland, Edinburgh    46

National Portrait Gallery, London    36, 49, 56

The National Trust, Ickworth    83

The National Trust, Polesden Lacey    32

The National Trust for Scotland    24

Phoenix Assurance Company Ltd    16

Private collections    10, 11, 15, 23, 26, 27, 58, 61, 67, 74, 77, 87, 88, 89

John and Mable Ringling Museum of Art, Sarasota, Florida    25

Royal College of Physicians    45

Fine Arts Museums of San Francisco    57

Major John Shirley    51

Earl Spencer    86

The Countess of Sutherland    34

The Trustees of the Tate Gallery    69

The Marquess of Tavistock and the Trustees of the Bedford Estates    40

Sir John R. H. Thouron, KBE    68

Mrs Montagnie Van Norden    70

Musée National du Château de Versailles et Trianon    44

Victoria and Albert Museum    65

The Duke of Wellington    76

Wellington Museum, Apsley House    30

The Marquess of Zetland    14

We are grateful to all owners for kindly allowing their pictures to be reproduced in this catalogue.
No.31, The Hon Shute Barrington, Bishop of Durham, is reproduced by kind permission of the Lord Bishop of Durham; copyright reserved to the Church Commissioners for England and the Courtauld Institute of Art.

# Index of Sitters and Subjects